OPEN ROAD'S BEST OF COSTA RICA

5th Edition

Charlie Morris & Bruce Morris

OPEN ROAD TRAVEL GUIDES –
*designed for the amount of time you **really** have for your trip!*

Open Road Publishing

Open Road's new travel guides.
Designed to cut to the chase.
You don't need a huge travel encyclopedia – you need a selective
guide to steer you right. If you're going on vacation for a few
weeks or less, get a guide that brings you the best of any destination for the amount of time you really have for your trip!

Open Road – the guide you need for the trip you want.

The New Open Road Best Of Travel Guides.
Right to the point.
Uncluttered.
Easy.

5th Edition

Open Road Publishing
www.openroadguides.com

Text Copyright © 2014 by Charlie Morris & Bruce Morris
- All Rights Reserved -
ISBN 13: 978-1-59360-201-7
Library of Congress Control Number: 2014940430

For photo credits and acknowledgments, turn to page 239.

Contents

9. THE CENTRAL PACIFIC COAST 154

1. INTRODUCTION

Costa Rica is a tropical paradise with the comforts of civilization. **All the wonderful attractions of the tropics are here**: sun-soaked beaches, azure seas, laughing monkeys, brightly-colored flowers and birds, the magical sound of palm fronds rustling in a gentle breeze. Many of the hassles that plague other tropical destinations are absent, or at least much less severe. Costa Rica is far less poor than her neighbors, and that means less crime and fewer aggressive hustlers. Tourist facilities are well developed. You'll have no problems getting around the country by small plane or rented car, finding excellent lodgings with all the modern amenities, and enjoying delightful local or international cuisine.

Costa Rica welcomes a huge number of visitors every year, and most come to experience her vast treasury of natural wonders. The rain forests hold **a stunning array of flora and fauna** (to give just one example, Costa Rica has more species of birds than the entire continent of North America), from playful monkeys to gaudy scarlet macaws to elusive wild cats. The seas teem with tropical fish. The volcanoes show nature at her most spectacular. There's a vast variety of landscapes, from sparkling beaches to coastal swampland to high mountains carpeted with lush greenery.

The greatest asset of this peaceful and serene country is **her people**. The natives, called "Ticos," are some of the friendliest folks you'll meet anywhere. They've built a relatively prosperous nation, which has had a stable democracy for longer than any other Latin American country, and which has avoided the civil wars that have plagued her neighbors. Costa Rica has the best and most peaceful government of any country south of Canada. The **activities are endless**. Fishing is spectacular, from tarpon and snook on the Caribbean coast to billfish in the Pacific. Surfing conditions are some of the best in the world, and kiteboarders find constant breezes on Lake Arenal. The rivers offer breathless whitewater rafting and peaceful wildlife-observation trips through the jungle. The **beautiful mountain landscapes** are perfect for hiking, horseback riding and mountain biking.

Of course, many travelers also enjoy more sedate pursuits, such as sipping a cool drink while basking on a beautiful beach, and the opportunities for doing that in Costa Rica are second to none.

2. OVERVIEW

Costa Rica has a **huge variety of astonishing scenery** and climates for such a small country. You can visit the volcanoes and cloud forests of the central highlands, then explore the pristine beaches of the Pacific, all on the same trip. There are all kinds of fun activities for all interests and all levels of strenuousness. If you want to get deep in the jungle and be an ecotourist, or if your tastes run to action sports such as surfing, kiteboarding, diving, fishing or whitewater rafting, you can find the trip of a lifetime here. Along the way, you'll find pleasant and comfortable accommodations, sophisticated cuisine, exotic nightlife and a bit of shopping.

San José

Although there are a few things of interest in the capital city of San José, the main attractions for visitors to Costa Rica are found outside the cities. Even though it lacks the worst sort of third world slums and poverty, San José is basically an unattractive city with few tourist diversions. Since most flights from North America arrive in San José in the afternoon, usually too late to catch a flight or drive to more salubrious areas of the country, most visitors find themselves spending at least one night in town.

Tip: Although there are some good hotels in town, more peaceful and pleasant hotels and lodges can be found in the suburbs and further out, some convenient to the airport.

The Central Valley

The Central Valley is a green patchwork of coffee plantations, tropical forests and well-ordered farms, dotted with small cities. It's here that most of the population, and almost all of the industry, are concentrated. There are numerous things of interest for tourists within the Central Valley, including volcanoes, waterfalls, whitewater rafting, coffee plantations, rain forest tours, butterfly farms and other wildlife viewing opportunities.

North Caribbean Coast

The northeast of the country is a wild and roadless region of lowland marshes and jungles. Here you'll find some of the world's finest and most colorful fishing camps. Anglers battle it out with enormous tarpon and snook. Lovers of wildlife can take a jungle cruise through **Tortuguero National Park** or **Barra del Colorado National Wildlife Refuge**. The wild and deserted beaches of the region are important nesting sites for four different species of sea turtles.

South Caribbean Coast

South of the city of Limón, you'll find some of the most spectacular beaches in the country, and young people enjoying the Jamaican-flavored lifestyle. The area around **Cahuita** and **Puerto Viejo** offers excellent surfing, as well as beautiful coral reefs for diving and snorkeling. Remote wildlife reserves attract serious ecotourists.

North Central Region

The northern interior of Costa Rica includes some of her most famous sights. **Arenal** is one of the world's most active volcanoes. The nearby

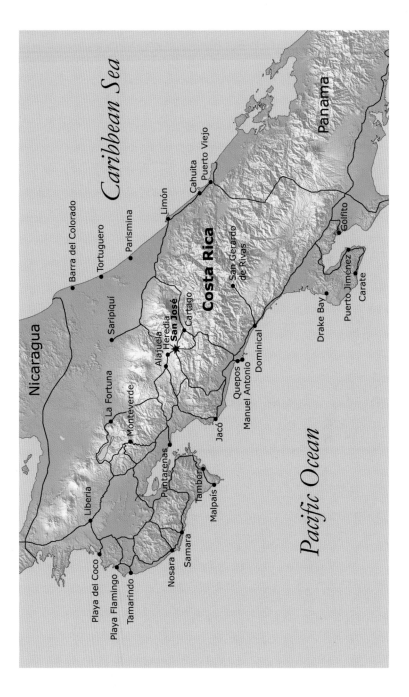

lake is one of the world's premier windsurfing and kiteboarding locales. **Monteverde Cloud Forest Preserve** is one of the country's most popular national parks. While this region is well trodden by tourist hordes, it's not hard to escape the crowds and get off the beaten path.

North Pacific Coast

The remote beaches of the **Nicoya Peninsula** are famous for both luxury resorts and down-to-earth hangouts for surfers and aging hippies. The climate is drier than in other parts of the country, but there are lots of lush tropical forests with wildlife and birds aplenty. Two highlights are **Santa Rosa National Park** at the northwest corner of the country, and the **Cabo Blanco** and **Curú Wildlife Refuges** at the tip of the peninsula.

Central Pacific Coast

The central Pacific region is convenient to San José, and attracts lots of visitors to the young beach town of **Jacó** and the more upscale beach/tropical forest area of **Manuel Antonio**. Tourists flock to the coast to surf, party, lounge around the pool with umbrella drinks, watch whales or view wildlife on hikes and jungle cruises. Honeymooners come to posh hotels that rival those of Hawaii. **Los Sueños Marina** and **Quepos** are known for some of the best fishing in the world for sailfish, marlin and dorado.

South Pacific Coast

The remote and relatively unspoiled **Osa Peninsula** is the best place in the country to view wildlife and primary rain forest. Jungle lodges accessible only by boat, plane or on foot cater to both luxury and backpacking travelers. Monkeys go about their business in the trees, as toucans and scarlet macaws fly about for all to see. Here you'll also find fantastic fishing and secret, spectacular surfing spots.

The Switzerland of Central America

This nickname was coined because of Costa Rica's relative affluence and lack of political violence, but it could also refer to the vast variety of terrain in such a small area (or, perhaps, the number of Swiss expatriates living in the country).

In a region that includes some of the Western Hemisphere's poorest nations, Costa Rica's economy, literacy rate and life expectancy compare favorably with those of so-called "first world" countries. Ticos enjoy state-funded medical insurance and a social security plan. Costa Rica's government has set an official goal of making the nation completely carbon neutral by 2021.

Although neighboring Nicaragua, El Salvador and Guatemala endured bloody civil wars in the late 20th Century, Costa Rica abolished its army in 1948. President Óscar Arias won the Nobel Peace Prize in 1987 for his help in ending the seemingly eternal civil unrest in the region.

Why is Costa Rica such a success story? Everyone has a pet theory, but in the final analysis, there seems to be no secret other than hard work and clean living or, as the Ticos would say, *pura vida*.

Wildlife

Partly thanks to its affluence and political stability, Costa Rica has done an excellent job of protecting its natural beauty and wildlife. National parks and nature reserves cover more than a quarter of the land area. This small country has a huge variety of different climates and ecosystems, and the parks have been planned to preserve at least a sample of each one. Although most wildlife is elusive, visitors can expect to see parrots, crocodiles, agoutis, coatis, monkeys, sloths, Jesus Christ lizards, and iguanas. The lucky may see anteaters, pacas, ocelots, dolphins or whales.

Bird Watching

With over 890 (and counting) bird species available for viewing, it is impossible for even the most hard-core birder to visit Costa Rica without adding significantly to their life list. Multicolored scarlet macaws and toucans, along with a wide assortment of Little Brown Birds (LBBs), flit through the forest, and vast flocks of seabirds patrol the coasts. If the birding gods smile on you, you may even see a quetzal, trogon, or ferruginous pygmy owl. Many lodges and tour companies cater specifically to birders.

Canopy Tours

Whether it is by zip line, elevated walkway or other means, tours of the rain forest canopy are all the rage. Most wildlife will be seen further away from such constructions and their herds of screaming tourists, so most canopy tours are not about wildlife and ecology: they are about having fun. Zipping through the trees while suspended from a cable is certainly an experience to treasure, and such experiences are available in most parts of the country.

Observing the Animals

The greatest thrill in Costa Rica is the chance to see **wild animals** going about their business in the forest. If you spend some time in the parks and preserves, your chances of seeing some critters are good. However, some animals are more easily seen than others, and some visitors have unrealistic expectations. Ring-tailed **coatis** (locally known as *pizotes*) are frequently seen, and they are friendly and fun. **Monkeys** are everyone's favorites, and they are pretty common (a little too common, say the owners of stolen sunglasses and hats). **Costa Rica has four species**: spider monkeys, white-faced capuchins, howlers, and the rare squirrel monkeys (*titis*). We'd all love to see a **wild cat**, and Costa Rica has several, including pumas, jaguars, ocelots, margays and jaguarundis. Outside of a zoo or rehabilitation center, however, you're unlikely to spot one of these secretive, nocturnal predators. If you want to see some of the rarer forest denizens, visit one the remote parks, walk quietly, and take your hikes in the early morning or just before dusk. I highly recommend hiring a local guide, who can show you animals (and plants) that you'd never see on your own.

Fishing

Fishing in Costa Rica is simply spectacular. The most hard-core fishing fanatic or the casual angler can't fail to be impressed with catches of more than 15 sailfish in one day, tarpon well over 100 pounds, snook over 15 pounds, and large hauls of more exotic species such as machaca and roosterfish. Tico fishing guides have learned the value of this fishy profusion in attracting tourists, and are dedicated to catch-and-release. Most of the action takes place in the northern Caribbean region (for tarpon and snook) and off the Pacific coast (for billfish and other offshore species).

Diving

The Caribbean coast has substantial areas of coral reefs—still in surprisingly good condition in spite of pollution, earthquake damage and fishing pressure. The Pacific side is not known for great visibility, but if you want to get close to manta rays, sharks and other large pelagic species, this is one of the best places in the world to do so. **Cocos Island**, located a few hundred miles out in the Pacific, is a world-class diving destination that's famous for huge schools of scalloped hammerhead sharks.

Tropical River Cruises

One of the very best ways to get close to wildlife (without getting out of breath) is to take a jungle cruise along the spectacular canals of the northern Caribbean area or through the mangroves of the central or southern Pacific. Colorful orchids and butterflies abound, and monkeys and crocodiles are close enough to touch (but don't).

Whitewater Rafting

A top global destination for whitewater rafting, Costa Rica offers several rivers suitable for all skill levels. The Pacuare and Reventazón are the most popular. Outfitters pick up and drop off at San José hotels for one-day or overnight expeditions.

Windsurfing & Kiteboarding

With steady winds of up to 30 mph, Lake Arenal is one of the top kiteboarding and windsurfing locations in the world, and the view is quite unique. Small lodges on the lakeside cater to all levels of skill.

Golf

Costa Rica has several championship courses, all with awesome mountain or ocean scenery. The Nicoya Peninsula boasts five spectacular seaside courses, most built in the 1990s by famous designers. Monkeys in the rough and crocodiles in the ponds add to the adventure. The new Four Seasons Hotel in Guanacaste has a beautiful Arnold Palmer course.

Surfing

The movie *Endless Summer* highlights a few of the more spectacular surfing destinations in Costa Rica. The north Pacific region is famous for the tubular break at **Witches Rock**, and the southern Pacific region boasts one of the longest waves in the world (1/4 mile) at **Pavones**. On the Caribbean side, surfing is concentrated in the south near **Puerto Viejo** and **Cahuita**. The **Salsa Brava** is known to be a world-class surfing challenge. Board rentals and instruction are widely available. The killer breaks and the totally awesome surf scene attract gnarly surfers from all over the world, dude!

Volcanoes

With dozens of cones to choose from, few visitors to Costa Rica escape seeing a volcano, sometimes in all their erupting glory. Just outside San José, bubbling hot **Poás** is easy to get to. The perfect cone of **Arenal** attracts thousands of visitors to its rain forest-shrouded slopes. **Rincón de la Vieja National Park** has nine cones and a huge variety of volcanic terrain.

Taking the Kids

Ticos love kids. Kids love the beach and anything to do with monkeys. Almost all of the most visited areas of the country have dozens of organized tours and activities appropriate for the whole family. The food and water are good and most restaurants have the chicken tenders and fried potatoes that kids love.

Costa Rica Facts

Location: Central America, between Nicaragua and Panama
Population: 4,696,000
Government: Democratic republic
Languages: Spanish, English (in Caribbean region), indigenous languages
Highest Point: Cerro Chirripó, 12,500 feet
Coastline: Caribbean, 132 miles; Pacific, 635 miles
Biodiversity: 230 mammal species, 893 bird species, 220 reptile species, 180 amphibian species, 35,000 insect species, 9,000 plant species
Life Expectancy: 78 years
Literacy: 96%
Poverty rate: 16%

Shopping

Champion shoppers agree that Costa Rica suffers in comparison to neighboring countries when it comes to good local handcrafts, but there are a few gems to be found. Tourist shops selling artsy stuff are plentiful, but many of the craft items come from Mexico or Guatemala. **Toucans made from every material** known to man seem to be the most common tourist trinket, followed closely by turtles made from the same stuff. **Coffee** and **rum** make good gifts for the folks back home. Both are best purchased in a local grocery store. The duty-free shop at the airport is not any cheaper. Prices in tourist shops around the country are usually higher.

Tico Cuisine

Restaurants aimed at tourists are not cheap—expect to pay about what you would in North America or a bit more. Typical Costa Rican restaurants are much less expensive and serve the same chicken, pork, beef, and fantastic seafood found in upscale tourist joints. Some of the lodges serve delightful dishes made from the freshest local seafood, vegetables and fruits. The level of hygiene is generally high, and upset stomachs from eating in local eateries are rare.

3. WILDLIFE OF COSTA RICA

If you love the natural world, and would like an opportunity to observe tropical animals and plants in their natural habitat, then Costa Rica is the place for you. Because of its location and geography, Costa Rica has an **astounding variety of wildlife**. Because of the people's wise decisions, they have managed to preserve far more of this wealth in its natural state than have most countries.

Within the borders of this small nation are hundreds of mammal, bird, reptile and amphibian species; tens of thousands of insect species; and countless thousands of plant species (and this is just what's been described so far: when it comes to plants and small invertebrates, there are thought to be thousands more that scientists haven't gotten around to classifying yet).

With **dozens of national parks, refuges and reserves of various kinds**, the critters have plenty of space to roam around, and you are welcome to pay them a visit. Much of the tourist industry is built around showing off the country's natural wonders. Dozens of wilderness lodges and tour operators are at your disposal to help you get a glimpse of those exotic animals and plants.

At most parks, you're welcome to wander about on your own, but it's well worth the money to **hire a local guide** (which you can do at park ranger stations or through your lodge). With a guide, you'll learn much more about the local ecosystem, and probably see animals you would never have seen on your own. At some parks, going with a guide is your only option, as some are accessible only by boat, and a few restrict access to protect the animals.

Costa Rica has many different habitats, including rain forest, cloud forest, dry forest, marshes and mangrove swamps. Each has its own unique ecosystem, and its own set of inhabitants. For various reasons, some animals are much more commonly seen than others. To increase your chances of animal sightings, walk quietly in the forest, and take your hikes in the early morning or just before dusk, when animals are more active. I highly recommend hiring a local guide, who can point out animals that you would never see on your own. Sloths, for example, are hard to spot unless you know what you're looking for—to you or me, they tend to look like a lump of moss on a branch.

Here are some of the wild creatures you may hope to see.

Mammals

The **ring-tailed coati** (*nasua nasua*), which the Ticos call a *pizote* (pronounced pee-SOH-tay), is a cute and gregarious creature with a long tail and a prehensile nose, which it uses to snuffle among the leaf litter on the forest floor for bugs, small lizards and frogs.

You're almost certain to see at least a few *pizotes,* as they are quite common, diurnal (active during the day), and not particularly shy. On the contrary, at some of the more frequented parks, where people have been feeding them, you may be accosted by bands of them begging for goodies. Their antics can be amusing, but you really shouldn't feed them or any other wild animals.

Costa Rica also has **raccoons** (*procyon lotor*), the same as the familiar North American variety. They occupy much the same niche as the *pizotes,* but are active at night. Another commonly seen forest dweller is the **agouti**, which looks something like a large brown guinea pig.

Costa Rica has four species of monkeys, three of which are found throughout the country. The most common is the playful **spider monkey** (*ateles geoffroyi*). You may also see the **white-faced capuchin** (*cebus capucinus*). The large black **howler monkeys** (*alouatta palliate*) make a loud noise that sounds less like howling than like the barking of a large dog. Even if you don't see them, you're sure to hear them far off in the forest.

The smallest and most exotic primate is the Central American **squirrel monkey** (*saimiri oerstedii*), which the locals call *mono titi.* This furry little goblin lives only in a small swath of coastal habitat from around Quepos on the Pacific coast down into the northern bit of Panama. Manuel Antonio National Park and the Osa Peninsula are the places to see *titis.*

Sloths are not rare, but are tough to spot in the forest, at least without a local guide. There are two varieties, the **two-toed** (*choloepus hoffmanni*) and the **three-toed** (*bradypus variegatus*). Sloths spend most of their time in trees snoozing, inching along branches at a snail's pace, and eating leaves. Ironically, their slow and sedentary ways protect them from predators. It's not only humans who tend to mistake a sloth for a lump of moss on a branch. Manuel Antonio National Park is stiff with sloths.

The very patient may catch a glimpse of some of the rarer mammals, including **tapirs, anteaters, peccaries, coyotes, foxes**, and the **tayra**, a sleek weasel-like carnivore. **River otters** are especially fascinating to watch. Small forest mammals range from exotic ones such as the **kinkajou** (*potos flavus*) to more mundane species such as **porcupines, armadillos, skunks** and dozens of species of rodents. There are eight species of **opossum** and well over 100 species of **bats**!

Costa Rica has no less than **six wild cats**. The kings of the jungle are the magnificent **spotted jaguar** (*panthera onca*) and the **puma** (*puma concolor*), a tawny relative of the North American cougar and Florida panther. Smaller felines are the beautiful little **spotted ocelot** (*leopardus pardalis* – *see photo below*), the **margay** (*leopardus wiedii*), and the rare **tigrillo** (or *oncilla*), no bigger than a house cat (*leopardus tigrinus*). The slightly larger **jaguarundi** (*herpailurus yaguarondi*) looks like a strange cross between a weasel and a cat.

The puddy-tats are fairly rare, mostly nocturnal, and very shy of people. The likelihood of seeing one in the wild is almost nil, unless you spend a good bit of time at one of the more remote lodges. If you are lucky enough to see a feline, you will probably see it from behind, rapidly fleeing from your headlights, as I did one dark night in the Osa Peninsula. There are a number of small zoos (Zoo Ave in Alajuela) and rehabilitation centers (Proyecto Asis, near Arenal) where you can see captive cats.

Don't Overlook the Small Stuff

We all want to see something cool, such as a large mammal or an exotic bird. But this isn't a TV show, and the critters don't always perform on schedule. Don't obsess about trophy sightings and miss the less glamorous, but fascinating, beauty all around. Trees, flowers, lush tropical greenery, fruits and spices, butterflies and all kinds of interesting bugs (take a night hike to see some really exotic creepy-crawlies) are easy to see, going about their business unnoticed by humans who rush by, searching for the elusive quetzal.

Reptiles & Amphibians

Snappy saurians may make you think twice about swimming in the rivers. The bridge at Tárcoles, which you'll cross shortly before reaching the Pacific coast from San José, is famous for the shoals of pointy-nosed **crocodiles** in the river below. You'll see the smaller **caimans** on almost any river boat ride. There's a huge variety of **snakes** (130 species), including **boa constrictors**, the bright yellow **eyelash palm pit viper**, the **fer-de-lance** (or *terciópelo*), one of the world's deadliest snakes, and the **bushmaster**, the world's largest pit viper, which can grow to 10 feet long and is locally called *matabuey* (ox killer)! Watch your step in the forest, but don't worry—snakebites are rare.

There's a variety of brightly-colored frogs, some of which are called **poison-arrow frogs** because the local Indians make poison arrows from them. According to legend, if you lick one you'll get high, but I'd stick to rum if I were you. Notable lizards include enormous **green iguanas**, and the **Jesus Christ lizard**, named for its ability to "walk on water" by skipping quickly across the surface.

Birds

The variety of birds is simply amazing, and so is the number of people who come to Costa Rica for the sole purpose of seeing them (the birds, that is). As this small country has more bird species than most continents, birders (or **twitchers**, as the English call them) have plenty of opportunities to add species to their **life lists**. Only a true birder can understand the excitement of seeing **LBBs** (Little Brown Birds) such as the tinamou,

Audubon's shearwater, wedge-rumped storm petrel, fulvous-whistling duck, great potoo and buffy-crowned wood partridge.

Everyone, however, loves such flamboyant fliers as **toucans** (six species), **hummingbirds** (between 50 and 60 varieties, each more brightly colored than the last) and Costa Rica's iconic bird, the **scarlet macaw**. These very large members of the parrot family are, despite the name, arrayed in all the colors of the rainbow. You'll see them throughout the southern half of the country, munching out in the almond trees (their images you'll see everywhere, on t-shirts, fridge magnets et al). Some birds have attained mythic status, like the **trogon**, the resplendent **quetzal**, the **harpy eagle** and the **curassow**, a ground bird that looks something like a well dressed turkey. At night, you may see one of the many stately species of owls. Coastal regions teem with majestic herons (including the rufescent tiger heron), egrets, ibises, storks, spoonbills, cormorants and other shorebirds.

Flora
Plant lovers will likewise be in Heaven. Here are thousands of exotic plant species. Visitors from subtropical climes will find familiar plants gone wild—have you ever seen a palm tree with a 10-foot diameter trunk and 30-foot-long fronds?

The tropical rain forest has many more species of trees than its temperate counterpart. Whereas a typical North American forest is dominated by only a few species of trees, Costa Rican forests have thousands. Many produce edible fruits or other useful products. A few are dangerous, like the **manzanillo tree**, locally called *el hinchador,* which has a caustic latex sap. Flowering trees such as the **jacaranda** add seasonal splashes of color.

Epiphytes (plants that grow on other plants) such as **orchids** (*orquídeas* [or-KEE-day-oss] in Spanish) and **bromeliads** occupy every available square inch in the dripping, humid cloud forest. There are over 1,500 species of orchids here, and the country is a major supplier to the garden trade. Costa Rica's national flower is the **purple orchid** (*cattleya skinneri*), a very gaudy variety that blooms mainly in March and April. Orchids are

not so easy to view in the wild, as most grow high up in trees. Fortunately, there are plenty of opportunities to see them in botanical gardens.

In fact, if you're interested in plants of any kind, I highly recommend a visit to one of the many botanical gardens throughout the country.

The species are all neatly labeled, and you'll learn a lot about fruit trees and other cultivated plants that you aren't likely to see in the rain forest. Hummingbirds and butterflies are frequent visitors. You can find a list of botanical gardens throughout the country at: *www.mapcr.com.*

Dozens of wild and crazy fruits are available, both whole and fresh-squeezed. Whether familiar fruits such as **mangos, papayas** and **pineapples** (which are much sweeter and juicier here than the mass-shipped varieties you find at the supermarket in Des Moines) or exotic varieties such as **mamotes, pejibayes, chiverres** and **carambolas,** I highly recommend trying them whenever offered. Quench your thirst with a **pipa,** a chilled green coconut with a straw inserted so you can sip the sweet milk. Kids love to chew on a stalk of sugar cane.

What is Ecotourism, Anyway?

Ecotourism is a term you'll hear kicked around quite a bit on your travels. Most visitors are here to enjoy the natural wonders, but does that make us all ecotourists? Does spending a couple of hours in the forest with a herd of other gringos make you an ecotourist? Or must you spend a week helping with the research at one of the remote biological stations (for example Ecolodge San Luis, near Monteverde) to earn the title?

In fact, ecotourism is a state of mind, **an ideal of sustainable, minimally invasive tourism** that both visitors and those in the tourism industry should strive for (alas, both groups often fall short). Ecotourists leave no litter, don't feed or interfere with the animals, and consume only products that are harvested in a sustainable manner. A true eco-lodge recycles and conserves, releases no waste into the environment, uses renewable energy, and has as little impact on the natural habitat as possible. Ecotourism is also about preserving an important species called local workers. A central concept of ecotourism is the idea that local people can make a better living by helping tourists enjoy the rain forest than they could by chopping it down. Ecotourists patronize local businesses, and buy local products.

The International Ecotourism Society defines ecotourism as "responsible travel to natural areas that conserves the environment and improves the well-being of local people." Their web site at *www.ecotourism.org* includes lists of environmentally friendly lodges and tour operators. The Costa Rican Tourist Board rates hotels on a scale of one to five green leaves, based on how close they come to the ideal of sustainable tourism. Find out more at *www.turismo-sostenible.co.cr.*

Marine Life

The magnificent menagerie doesn't end at the water's edge. **Sea lions** live on the rocky Pacific coast, and **manatees** swim the mangrove estuaries of the Caribbean. Nine types of **dolphin** make their homes in Costa Rican waters, and several species of **whales**, including humpback, sperm, killer and pilot whales visit from time to time.

There are seven **sea turtle** species in the world, and five of them nest on Costa Rica's beaches. Female sea turtles return year after year to the beaches where they were born, and lay their eggs in the sand. When the babies hatch, they scamper to the sea en masse.

Watching the turtles do their thing on the beaches has turned into something of a New Age religious ritual for some. The folks who make the yearly pilgrimage here during spawning season are quite different from the birder crowd, but are just as fanatical. The hottest turtle-worship spots are Tortuguero on the Caribbean coast, where **hawksbill**, **loggerhead**, **green** and **leatherback sea turtles** nest; and isolated Playa Nancite in Santa Rosa National Park on the Pacific, one of the few known nesting sites for the rare olive ridley. See the regional sections to find out what time of year the turtles are laying.

Some of the most impressive ocean wildlife can be seen beneath the surface. Costa Rica is considered one of the top advanced diving destinations

in the world, not for the usual coral reefs, but rather for the large pelagic species that frequent her waters. The Caribbean coast has a few areas of coral reef (notably in Cahuita National Park and the Gandoca-Manzanillo National Wildlife Refuge), and the northern Pacific coast has some fine reefs as well. However, the main draw for divers is the chance to mingle with schools of **tuna**, **sea turtles**, giant **manta rays** and several species of **sharks**, including the huge but harmless whale shark and several species of potential man-eaters such as hammerheads and bull sharks. You may also get to swim with dolphins and, on rare occasions, whales.

This Pacific diving is advanced diving: deep dives far offshore, with rough seas and currents to contend with, to say nothing of the difficulty of keeping your composure around huge fish that could gulp you down like an olive.

The crown jewel of Costa Rican diving is **Cocos Island**, an uninhabited isle located a long 480-km boat ride southwest of the mainland, which Jacques Cousteau named as one of the most beautiful places in the undersea world. The entire island is a national park—it's covered by virgin forest and ringed by coral reefs. Here you may see all sorts of large pelagic species, including enormous schools of **scalloped hammerhead sharks**. The only way to get there is on a weeklong trip on one of two liveaboard dive boats.

Anglers haul in a vast variety of species. Familiar game species such as **sailfish**, **marlin**, **tuna**, **wahoo**, **jack**, **tarpon**, **snook**, **snapper**, **grouper** and **dorado** (the local name for the colorful and delicious fish also known as dolphin or mahi-mahi) are plentiful and large. Those with a taste for the exotic can target several types of shark, as well as a couple of fish found only in the region. The **roosterfish** is a large member of the jack family that's quite colorful, with a resplendent dorsal crest. Like all of its clan, it's a hard battler. Other local fish include the **machaca** and the freshwater **guapote**, a colorful little cichlid that's quite a fighter. **Sawfish** browse among the mud bottoms of the canals.

To learn more about Costa Rican wildlife, read the comprehensive *Costa Rica: The Ecotraveller's Wildlife Guide* by Les Beletsky; the pocket-sized *Costa Rican Wildlife: An Introduction to Familiar Species* by James Kavanagh; or *A Guide to the Birds of Costa Rica* by F. Gary Stiles. For those of a scientific disposition, NatureServe (*www.natureserve.org/infonatura*) has a searchable database of every species of bird, mammal, and amphibian found in Costa Rica (and neighboring countries).

4. SAN JOSÉ & THE CENTRAL VALLEY

For most visitors, Costa Rica's capital is a staging area for trips to the rain forests and the coasts. However, you're quite likely to end up staying at least one night in the area, as most flights to Costa Rica arrive late in the day, not leaving enough time to drive or fly to another part of the country. Why not make a virtue of necessity and have some fun?

Visit the **Central Market** and a couple of the city's small museums, and then take a trip to a volcano or a coffee plantation. In the evening, enjoy the amenities of one of the most cosmopolitan capitals in Central America.

Costa Rica's capital city is a sprawling metropolis—the greater urban area has over a million inhabitants. In Spanish colonial days, the capital was located in nearby Cartago, and San José was a sleepy village. Shortly after Costa Rica became independent from Spain in 1821, president Juan Mora Fernández moved the government to San José in order to symbolize a clean break with the past. Its comparatively recent history explains why San José has little in the way of grand colonial architecture (but suburbs such as **Cartago**, **Heredia** and **Alajuela** do). The local nickname for San José is *Chepe* (pronounced CHE-pe).

HIGHLIGHTS

• **Poás Volcano** – See a genuine bubbling volcano just a short ride from San José.

• **Coffee Plantation Tour** – See how much of the population of the Central Valley make their living, and where your morning cuppa comes from.

• **Zoo Ave** – At this delightful small zoo, not far from the airport, you can see all the animals you missed in the rain forest.

Don't try to drive around central San José, which features the usual Central American anarchy: treacherous potholes, very few street signs, and hordes of over-exuberant drivers on everything from tiny scooters to huge trucks to the odd mule cart.

The local bus system is decent, so during the day it's practical to use it to get into town from your hotel. Better yet, taxis are cheap, and have the added benefit that you don't have to figure out how to get to where you're going. Local drivers are helpful, and usually know a smattering of English. At night, a taxi is the safest way to get around.

Once out of town, you should have no problems driving—the main roads are generally well maintained. Do be sure to obtain a good map, however. You can rent a car at the airport and get right on the **Interamerican Highway**, which runs the length of the country (it's also called Highway One north of San José, and Highway Two to the south).

COORDINATES

San José, the capital and largest city of Costa Rica, lies in a mountain valley in the central part of the country. Here you'll find the international airport, and connections to the main north-south highway. The city is divided into 11 districts.

SAN JOSÉ IN A DAY

Stay at a nice hotel out in the green suburbs, and take a local bus into central San José for the morning. In one day you can see the few highlights Costa Rica's capital city has to offer, and still have time to explore the area outside San José's city limits as well.

Morning

The **Parque Central** (Central Park) is one of the main hubs for city buses, so let's head there. The small park is a refuge from the noisy, hectic city center. If it's a Sunday morning, you might catch an outdoor concert.

A couple of blocks down Avenida 2, the **Teatro Nacional** (National Theater) is a local landmark that people will probably tell you to see. It's interesting enough to merit a quick look if you're in the area. The Neoclassical facade, with its statues of Beethoven and allegorical figures such as Comedy, Tragedy, Dance, Music, and Fame, is reminiscent of the great opera houses of Europe, but

the indoor paintings of the coffee and banana harvests, and the wonderful parquet flooring, are purely Costa Rican. Just across the street is the **Café**

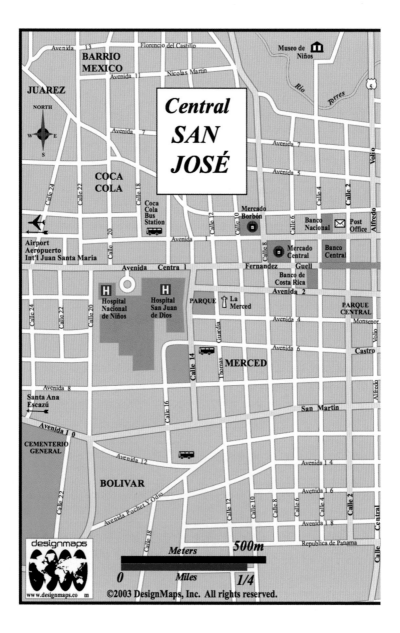

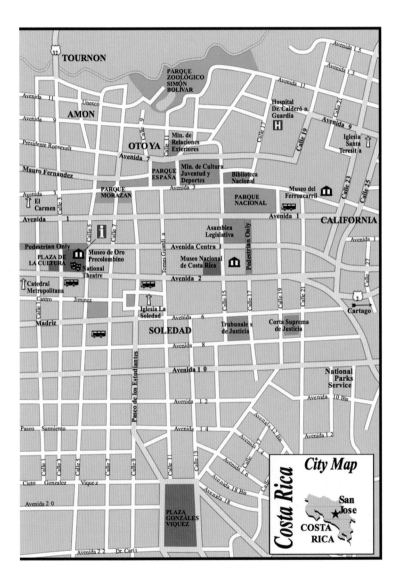

Parisienne, a welcoming little sidewalk café that makes the perfect San José people-watching spot.

Stroll north along the **Avenida Central**, which at this point is a pedestrian mall lined with small shops, department stores and fast food restaurants. Between Calles 3 and 5 is a parky square called the **Plaza de la Cultura** (Plaza of Culture). The **Pre-Columbian Gold Museum** and, just around the corner, the **Fidel Tristan Jade Museum**, are each worth a quick look. If you walk east along Avenida Central a few blocks, you will come to a shopping area with stalls selling a complete array of tourist trinkets, toucans and t-shirts. *Info: Pre-Columbian Gold Museum: Avenida Central and Calle 5, open daily 9:15am-4:30pm. Entry $11. www.museosdelbanco-central.org/eng; Tel. 2243-4202. Fidel Tristan Jade Museum: 7th Avenue, between 11th and 9th Streets, open Mon-Fri 8:30am-3:30pm; Sat 10am-2pm. Entry $7. Tel. 2287-6034.*

A few blocks from the Plaza of Culture, up the hill called the **Cuesta de Moras**, is the **Bellavista Fortress** (look for the bullet holes, a legacy of the 1948 civil war). This impressive colonial fortress towers over the city and houses the **Muséo Nacional** (National Museum). Here you'll find another collection of fine pre-Columbian art objects, as well as pottery and jewelry from every region of the country, exhibits depicting events in Costa Rican history, and a butterfly garden. *Info: Between Avenida Central and Avenida 2, open Tue-Sat 8:30am-4:30pm; Sun 9am-4:30pm. Entry $8. www.museo-costarica.go.cr; Tel. 2257-1433.*

It's getting towards time for lunch, so let's head for the **Mercado Central** (Central Market), at Calle 6 and Avenida 1. This bustling indoor market is a maze of stalls selling local crafts, clothing, flowers, meat, fish, vegetables, tropical spices and every little thing a Tico or a tourist might need. Also

Safety Tips

San José has plenty of **pickpockets**. An internal money belt (the kind that fits under your shirt) is a good idea. An external "fanny pack" is a very bad one—an irresistible temptation for thieves. Be alert, especially in the crowded streets **around the Central Market**. Crooks aren't the only hazard. **Sidewalks are in poor repair** in San José (and other cities), so watch your step. And be very careful crossing streets—drivers tend to have little regard for pedestrians.

in here are several little *sodas* (cafés) where you can grab an inexpensive and tasty lunch, perhaps a *casado* with fish, rice and beans.

¿Y para tomar? To drink? Exotic fruit smoothies are popular in Costa Rica and are often served with lunch. Stop by a little stall and cool down with a glass of mango, papaya or *piña* (pineapple), or just point to the most brightly colored jug.

The **excellent local coffee** is available any time. Don't miss tasting one of Costa

Rica's delicious beers. **Imperial** is tasty without being overpowering. **Bavaria Negra** is a robust dark beer.

Afternoon

In the afternoon, head out to **Alajuela**, one of the most pleasant of San José's many suburbs, near the airport (Alajuela is also a convenient and enjoyable place to find a hotel—see *Best Sleeps*). The main square is shaded by mango and palm trees, and surrounded by some splendid but faded colonial-era mansions. If you look closely, you may see some of the resident two-toed sloths (and possible some slothful humans lying about).

Just outside Alajuela, along the highway to Atenas, is the **Zoo Ave**, which is dedicated to reintroducing rehabilitated endangered species to the wild, particularly scarlet macaws. The large park is home to over 100 bird species and dozens of mammals and reptiles. In contrast to the San José city zoo, it is modern, clean and neat. The animals roam around in large, semi-open enclosures and little signs tell you the names of the tropical plants that fill the park.

You can get very close (almost too close at times) to monkeys (all four native species), pumas, tapirs, toucans, parrots (13 species) and other tropical creatures. Zoo Ave is well worth a visit, either at the beginning or end of your trip. I stop by over and over again. This is a great place to visit with kids. It's also an especially nice spot for photographers, who can get shots of many forest denizens with no intervening bars or fences. Scarlet macaws pose regally and monkeys cavort.

Tip: Don't hang around directly under a tree with monkeys in it. Stand a few feet out of the drop zone, and you may get a good laugh, not only at the apes, but at the hapless tourists who didn't read this book! *Info: Open daily 9am-5pm. Admission $15. www.zooavecostarica.org; Tel. 2433-8989.*

Although it has recently had some slight improvements, the **zoo** in San José, near Barrio Amón, is sad. The few animals seem listless in their small and dirty surroundings. New management is expected to clean things up but it will take millions to make the zoo something to be proud of. Perhaps the city should close it completely.

Find Your Way in San José

Ticos seldom use street addresses as such. Instead, locations are described as "on the corner of…" or "in between…" particular streets. In San José (and several other cities), *calles* (streets) run north-south, and *avenidas* (avenues) run east-west. Many streets have no signs, so you may have to look for a street that does have a sign and count back (or forward) to the one you want.

Evening

You'll have no problem finding a nice place to eat. San José has a nice variety of restaurants, offering French, Italian, Swiss, Spanish, Mexican and Asian cuisine, not to mention some great seafood. The better ones are priced about the same as in the US (see *Best Eats*).

Escazú is a suburb of San José popular with expatriates, where you can find all the US chain restaurants such as Outback, Pizza Hut and the burger joints. Out here you'll also find a few nice hotels like the **Casa Cristal** and **Hotel Alta** that have wonderful restaurants open to the public.

San José's nightlife is quite a scene, with a full palette of bars and clubs, many featuring live music (see *Best Nightlife*). Of particular interest is the **Jazz Café** in San Pedro, which has good food and a nightly lineup of local and Central American performers. Do not walk around central San José at night. Take a taxi.

San José is famous for sex tourism. Certain bars teem with freelance (licensed and inspected) ladies of the night trolling for tourists with cash to spend on a pretty girl. So-called **Gringo Gulch** is the center for this action. The cornerstone is the interesting **Hotel del Rey** and the **Blue Marlin Bar** in its lobby (see *Best Sleeps*). As in most of the world, prostitution is legal and regulated by the authorities. Having sex with anyone under 18, however, is strictly illegal.

A FANTASTIC WEEKEND IN THE CENTRAL VALLEY

If you have two or three days to spend in the San José area, use it as a base for visiting the attractions of the surrounding area. It's preferable to stay in the quieter, more wholesome suburbs just outside San José, as the city center has few attractions or activities that are likely to occupy you for more than one day.

The Central Valley has dozens of tours and excursions to choose from, lasting from an hour or two visiting a coffee plantation to overnight trips for rafting, fishing or cloud forest exploration. Short trips to more remote parts of the country are also feasible, thanks to small planes and an extensive network of landing strips, but you needn't travel far from San José to see volcanoes and rain forests, or get into various adventure sports. Most tour operators can include transportation to and from your hotel door.

Almost any hotel will help you book tours. You can, of course, book tours directly on your own or use one of these two tour operators that I like:

- **Costa Rica Expeditions** in downtown San José. *Info: www.costaricaexpeditions.com; Tel. 2257-0766, 2521-6099.*
- **Costa Rica Outdoors** in Santa Ana. *Info: www.costaricaoutdoors.com; Tel. 2231-0306, 2231-0673 or 800/308-3394 US.*

Many companies offer combination tours. You can combine a visit to a volcano with a visit to a butterfly farm, followed by a tour of a coffee *beneficio*, or processing plant, with a stop somewhere for lunch. These combinations are a great idea, although some of the more strenuous activities, such as rafting, may leave you ready for a cold drink, dinner and bed at an early hour.

Rafting

One-day or overnight rafting trips on the **Pacuare** and **Reventazón** rivers are a great way to get out of town, see the rain forest, and get your adrenalin going. Outfitters such as **Costa Rica Expeditions** (see above) and **Ríos Tropicales** specialize in rafting and organize everything, picking you

up at your hotel in the morning and taking you to the put-in point in small tourist buses. Their rustic riverside lodges cook up hearty meals. *Info: www.riostropicales.com; Tel. 2233-6455, 866/722-8273 US.*

Either river can be covered in a one-day tour, but going overnight gives you a little more time on the river, and a chance to enjoy the tropical forest surroundings that tend to go by in a blur when you're racing through the rapids. Yes, you will get wet, but dry bags are provided so you can protect certain belongings. You won't need much more than a change of clothes.

Poás Volcano National Park

Just outside of town, **Poás Volcano National Park** is easy to get to, and well worth a look. The 2,708-meter volcano is quite active, although the last major eruption took place in 1954.

This is probably Costa Rica's most easily accessible volcano. You can drive almost to the rim itself and walk the rest of the way on a paved pathway. You can't go around the crater more than a short way, but there is a nice observation platform, and there is almost always some bubbly action going on.

Poás is one of the few volcanic craters in the world you can get to without getting out of breath. It is only a short walk on a nice smooth path from the car park to the crater rim. You will probably see a few *pizotes* cadging handouts. Don't fall for their pitch: just keep on walking and try not to let them catch your eye. There is also a small crater lake you can see after a

walk through the forest, but go for the walk itself—the lake is only a mild attraction since it dried up last year.

Be sure you schedule your trip to Poás for **early in the morning**, as clouds (and crowds) start to move in and obscure the view of the crater as early as 10am. Bring a jacket, as it can be quite cold and windy up here. The visitor center is worth a look and has a small cafeteria and souvenir shop. You can, of course, get a nice cup of coffee. Try the tamales. They have the same toucan fridge magnets here that they have anywhere, so you may as well go ahead and buy here if you see something you like. *Info: The visitor center is open 8am-4pm. Entry: $10 adults. Tel. 2442-7041, 2430-4127.*

Note: Occasionally the park is closed due to too much bubbly action. In 2006 Poás was going through a stage of mild activity, blorping out gobs of extremely hot mud and gases in the general direction of the viewing platform usually occupied by gawking tourists. Call ahead to avoid disappointment or scalding.

Coffee Tours

Two coffee farms/processing plants (known as *beneficios*), **Britt** and **Doka**, are open to the public and offer organized tours. Both are just outside San José, and either one would make a great visit to combine with a trip to Poás or to the waterfalls. A trip to a *beneficio* is a must do for all visitors to Costa Rica.

Café Britt is the big name in coffee in Costa Rica, and visitors see it advertised, served and sold everywhere. Cute little bags of their interesting coffee are on offer to tourists wherever they roam. The java is excellent, and the tour of their facilities just outside Heredia is quite a production.

Coffee is the world's second-most traded commodity (after oil). The coffee trade is important not only for local communities in countries such as Costa Rica, but also for the global environment, as rain forest is often cleared to make space for coffee plantations (to say nothing of its importance in getting millions of people up in the morning).

Coffee beans require extensive processing before they're ready to brew up a cup (no, you can't pick your own beans and brew a shot on the spot). The tour shows you each step of the process, from planting to picking to classifying, peeling, soaking, fermenting, sun drying and roasting.

Nearby **Doka Estate**, a worthy competitor to Britt, also offers an informative tour of their fields and traditional processing operations. Their coffee often trumps the more famous Britt in tasting competitions. Look for their **Tres Generaciones** brand. Tours are offered daily, and they have several packages available, with or without lunch and transportation.

At both establishments, you can order coffee and have it shipped home. It's actually fairly economical to buy coffee this way and have it shipped back. You'll pay more at home for regular old coffee! Any large grocery store in Costa Rica is a fine place to buy local coffee (although the Britt factory store is still the best deal in town). Duty free shops at the airport are no cheaper, and the selection in grocery stores is much better. *Info: Café Britt: www.coffeetour.com; Tel. 2277-1600, 800/GO BRITT US. $20 for the 90-minute "classic" tour, $47 for a more extensive "coffee lover's" tour, which includes lunch. Doka Estate: www.dokaestate.com; Tel. 2449-5152, 888/9 GO DOKA US.*

Heliconia Island

This **private botanical garden** is fairly small, but it's very well designed and is worth a visit, especially if you love flowers and/or bananas. Architect and graphic designer Tim Ryan laid out the five-acre gardens on an island in the Puerto Viejo River.

The namesake **heliconia** is a lovely tropical flower. Here are **70 different species** from all over the world, at least some of which are blooming year-round. The garden also features a huge variety of orchids, bromeliads, ferns, philodendrons, fruit trees, and some very rare palms. You can taste several varieties of bananas. The region has **over 400 bird species**: you may see not only rain forest denizens such as parakeets, trogons, toucans and tanagers, but water birds such as herons, egrets, kingfishers and kiskadees. Of course, hummingbirds and butterflies

are abundant. *Info: Heliconia Island is located 8 km from Puerto Viejo de Sarapiquí, about an hour north of San José. There's a nice but inexpensive bed & breakfast and an elegant restaurant. Open daily 8am-5pm. www.heliconiaisland.com; Tel. 2764-5220.*

La Paz Waterfall Gardens

Not too far from Poás, **La Paz Waterfall Gardens** has five spectacular waterfalls, which you can admire from an easy walking trail. A frothing white waterfall in the midst of lush green vegetation is one of the most photogenic scenes known to man. This large tourist park also has several other attractions. There's an **enormous enclosed structure with over 4,000 butterflies** flitting about (they claim it's the largest enclosed butterfly garden in the world, and I believe it). The hummingbird garden is also quite amazing, featuring 24 different species of these fascinating little aerobats. There are 3.5 km of walking trails, orchid houses, a small restaurant and a gift shop.

La Paz is not a cheap thrill, and it is far from undiscovered. But if you don't mind sharing the peace and quiet with a few busloads of other tourists, it makes a good visit to combine with other nearby attractions such as Poás or one of the coffee tours. Kids especially love the butterflies, some of which they can touch. *Info: Open 8am-5pm daily. Adults: $38; children 12 and under: $22. www.waterfallgardens.com; Tel. 2482-2720. There's also a hotel, called Peace Lodge, which has luxurious designer rooms that start around $315 double. www.waterfallgardens.com/about_peace_lodge.php.*

A WONDERFUL WEEK IN THE CENTRAL VALLEY

If you can spend a week in the San José area, as in the weekend plan, use it as a base for visiting even more of the Central Valley: volcanoes, parks, gardens, and coffee towns await!

Irazú Volcano National Park

In 1963, while President Kennedy was on a visit, Costa Rica's highest volcano, **Irazú**, blew its stack, sending clouds of muddy ash all over San José and the Central Valley. This kind of thing is said to be good for the coffee crop. At 3,432 meters (11,260 feet), it is still active from time to time and, although not quite as easy to get to as Poás, it is worth a visit if you fancy seeing what the surface of the moon looks like (according to astronaut Neil Armstrong). There are four craters to gaze at, and a bright green lake.

This is another attraction that you need to get to early in the morning, due to developing morning cloud cover. If the day is very clear (a rare occurrence) and you hold your mouth right, you might just be able to see both the Caribbean and Pacific coasts from up top. Irazú doesn't always have bubbly activity, but it makes a nice trip, and is a bit less touristed than Poás. *Info: Entry: $10 adults. Tel. 2200-5025.*

Braulio Carrillo National Park, Volcán Barva

Braulio Carrillo National Park is close to San José (12 miles), but is usually overlooked by tourists in a hurry to get to Monteverde and the "crowd forest." If you have driven from San José to the Caribbean coast along the main route, you may remember passing through an area of mountains lush, lush, lush with tropical foliage, dripping wet. This is Braulio Carrillo.

The park has two volcanoes and miles of tropical cloud forest. For quetzals (see photo on previous page), toucans, trogons, eagles, indeed **over 500 species of birds**, and the usual Costa Rican mix of mammals—monkeys, sloths, *pizotes* and maybe an ocelot—there is really no need to travel further. Every inch of space is covered with plants, including showy epiphytes such as orchids and bromeliads.

There are two ranger stations along the main highway, and each has **some good trails**. Another popular trail leads from the town of Sacramento to the crater of **Volcán Barva**, a dormant volcano, with several crater lakes. The park is huge, at over 21,000 acres (47,000 hectares), with many trails, some of them for serious campers willing to spend up to four days hiking in the mist. Guides are available through the park or through local lodges.

There is a lot of exploring to be done in this huge, but much-less-frequented cloud forest park. However, note that this park has an unfortunate reputation for crime. Always check in at the ranger station before setting out, consider hiring a local guide—and do not leave valuables in your car. *Info: Braulio Carrillo National Park is about 20 km northeast of San José. Buses stop right in front of the ranger stations. The main station is just past the southern entrance to the park. All three ranger stations are open 8am-4pm. Entry: $10 adults. Tel. 2261-2619.*

Busloads of tourists head for the **aerial tram**, just north of the park boundary. Here you can take pricey cable car rides through the forest canopy. *Info: www.rainforestadventure.com.*

Centro Neotrópico SarapiquíS

Yes, this place has a capital S at the end of its name! This research and educational center is run by a Belgian nonprofit organization, and includes a jungle lodge and three interesting attractions. The botanical garden has over 400 native plants, all neatly labeled, including epiphytes, orchids, ferns and various plants beloved of hummingbirds and butterflies. There's also a museum with exhibits on rain forest biology and the indigenous peoples of the region. Unlike some of its neighbors to the north, Costa Rica doesn't have very many Pre-Columbian archaeological sites. Here you'll find one of the best in the country. A **15th-century indigenous village** has been excavated and partially reconstructed, and there are some cool stone statues and **petroglyphs**. There's an upscale lodge with a pool (doubles are $120 per night, breakfast and taxes included) and a restau-

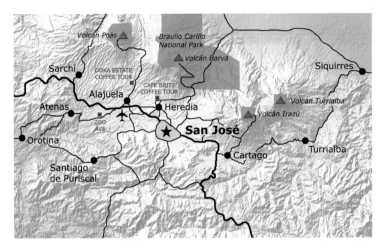

rant. *Info: Just off the main road near the village of La Virgen de Sarapiquí, about 85 km from San José. www.sarapiquis.org; Tel. 2761-1004.*

La Selva Biological Station

Operated by the Organization for Tropical Studies, La Selva is a reserve covering almost 3,900 acres (1,600 hectares) set aside for research. The research station allows a few visitors, who can share comfortable but rustic room and board with the researchers, and get a great rain forest tour with no crowds and very knowledgeable biologist guides. Keep an eye out for a tinamou, roseate spoonbill, curassow, band-tailed barbthroat or one of numerous LBBs (Little Brown Birds). Bring a raincoat, because the area averages well over a foot of rain per month. More than 240 scientific papers are published annually from research conducted at La Selva. *Info: www.ots.ac.cr; Tel. 2766-6565.*

BEST SLEEPS & EATS
BEST SLEEPS IN SAN JOSÉ

Most people who come to enjoy the tropical delights of Costa Rica arrive at the Juan Santamaría International Airport just outside San José on afternoon flights, without enough time to catch a local flight to their ultimate jungle, beach or other destination. Most internal flights leave in the morning to avoid afternoon cloud cover. This usually means a night spent more or less near the airport.

Although San José does have its attractions, in general one shouldn't feel guilty about blowing it off for more interesting places. San José has lots of nice hotels and restaurants but it tends to be noisy and exceedingly urban. There is not really much tropical charm.

Fortunately, the **suburbs and the Central Valley** around San José are much more laid-back and jungly, and are loaded with good places to stay and eat. Some of the best are conveniently near the airport for those who just need a place to stay overnight between planes. To enjoy the pleasures of the Central Valley, a lodge or hotel somewhat out of San José can be a good base for several days of exploration.

If you find you must stay in downtown San José, then here you are:

Aurola Holiday Inn $$$$
Right smack downtown, the Aurola has undergone an enormous remodeling job touching almost every feature of the hotel. It has now joined the Real Intercontinental as one of the best two business-oriented hotels in the area. It is a 17-story, hermetically sealed, big city business hotel with windows that don't open. The hotel would not be the least out of place in New York City or Los Angeles. The rooms on the upper floors have tremendous views of San José and the surrounding volcanoes.

One of the main advantages of the hotel is its location right downtown. It fronts on the Parque Morazán right in the center of town. There are 200 rooms and a presidential suite. The standard rooms have all the amenities expected: hair dryers, irons, wireless Internet connections, and piles of fluffy pillows. The suites are larger and are located on a floor with a business center, copy machine and a guest service attendant. The presidential suite is on the 16th floor with spectacular views over the city, an extra bedroom for bodyguard or nanny and a huge, luxurious, multi-room bathroom with Jacuzzi and sauna.

Hotel amenities include an indoor pool and jacuzzi, attractive casino, travel agency, beauty salon, convention facilities, meeting rooms of various configurations, underground parking, sauna, health spa, gym, gift shop and two restaurants. Another high-rise building with 22 floors is planned for next door which will contain extensive convention facilities, a big casino, a disco, a parking garage, and condos on top.

The 17th floor **El Mirador restaurant** (see *Best Eats*) cannot be beat for the awesome view over the city. Most of the tables are by the windows that wrap around three sides of the high rise. The atmosphere is piano-tinkling elegant with white shirt, bow tie waiters and a formal but charming Maitre D. It's not really any more expensive than other high-end eateries in town and the food is just fine. *Info: Calle 5, Avenida 5. www.aurolahotels. com; Tel. 2523-1000, 800/315-2621 US.*

BEST OF THE BEST –
OUR FAVORITE LODGING IN SAN JOSÉ
Hotel Grano De Oro $$$$

The Grano de Oro is truly a beautiful, unique hotel with loads of charm, and is very professionally run. The location is central, but it's on a quiet side street, so you miss most of the city noise and traffic. This is my first choice for a place to stay in town. It is a member of the **Small Distinctive Hotels of Costa Rica** trade association.

The rooms and suites are especially private. There is a luxurious suite near the roof with a large Jacuzzi and spectacular views of the city and surrounding mountains. Rooms are all unique—this is not a chain—this is a charming, boutique hotel with lots of character built in and around an old coffee baron's home, a maze of atriums and greenhouses with thousands of potted tropical plants, and lots of wrought iron and damask. Costa Rican artists handcrafted the art and furnishings.

The **restaurant is simply the best restaurant in town**, tending towards French with tropical infusions, orchestrated by Chef Francis Canal. The desserts are famous. The gift shop, although not large, is one of the better ones in San José. *Info: Calle 30, Avenidas 2/4. www. hotelgranodeoro.com; Tel. 2255-3322.*

Park Inn by Radisson $$$

Modern and soulless but comfortable, spotless and efficient, the 12-story Park Inn boasts fine views of the city, and is located within walking distance of the downtown market and museums, and a 20-minute taxi ride from the airport. The rooms are spacious, with comfortable beds and wonderful walk-in showers. The hotel has all the modern features you could wish for—free wireless internet, flat-screen TVs, a nice outdoor pool, a small fitness center.

The RBG Bar & Grill serves a nice breakfast buffet (included) until 10am, and fairly generic but good cuisine the rest of the day. The Park Inn is just around the corner from the Grano de Oro and its excellent restaurant (see above). By all accounts, the staff are friendly and efficient. *Info: Avenida 6, Calle 28. www.parkinn.com/hotel-sanjose; Tel. 2257-1011.*

Hotel Del Rey $$$

The five-story Neoclassical Hotel del Rey is listed as a National Heritage Treasure, but it's world-famous for more than its architecture. It is a clean, medium-quality hotel with elevator and central air. The ground floor bustles with a 24-hour casino, a crummy coffee shop/restaurant, and the more than lively bar.

The Del Rey is the San José stopover for guys on fishing junkets, and is the most popular hotel for men looking to hire women for an evening or longer.

At first glance, the **Blue Marlin Bar** beside the lobby is just a pleasant, US-style sports bar with reasonably priced drinks. But it won't take you long to notice the dozens (hundreds on the weekends) of freelance ladies of the evening hanging about. You have to see it to believe it, but leave the family in Carbondale. You can check out the action live from home on their webcam. The rooms are okay too. *Info: Avenida 1, Calle 9. www.delreyhotel.com; Tel. 2257-7800, 866/727-0270 US.*

BEST SLEEPS NEAR SAN JOSÉ

Attractive alternatives to city hotels are found in the villages and valleys and on the mountains and volcanic slopes around San José. Although surrounded by fruit orchards, coffee plantations and rain forests, the inns and lodges of the Central Valley are only minutes from downtown San José, and many are just a short ride from the international airport.

Having just said that, I may as well warn you that traffic between the airports and San José can be incredibly slow. There's a back road from Heredia to the Airport that's much quicker (20 to 25 minutes with moderate traffic).

Casa Turire $$$$

A member of **Small Distinctive Hotels of Costa Rica**, this is one of the most elegant hotels in the country. The 12 rooms and four suites feature graceful colonial-style décor, and luxury amenities such as hair dryers and private balconies. The restaurant serves Mediterranean cuisine with local organic ingredients and specialty  items. It is heavy with white linen and glassware.

A long, palm-lined entry drive leads to extensive grounds, tennis courts, a lovely spring-fed pool, and even a heliport. Casa Turire is close to the Irazú and Turrialba volcanoes, as well as the rather tame ruins at Guayabo National Monument. Located right on the Reventazón River, it would be a good luxury base for river rafting. *Info: www.hotelcasaturire.com; Tel. 2531-1111.*

Finca Rosa Blanca Country Inn $$$$

Gaudi and Timothy Leary must have inspired the architects for this unique, free-form white stucco property. "Elegant, yet whimsical," Finca Rosa Blanca is a very special luxury country inn in the coffee-covered hills not far outside San José. Sophisticated travelers will appreciate the attention to detail and over-the-top amenities.

If you don't mind spending for luxury and something different, you'll find Finca Rosa Blanca to be one of the nicest and most interesting places to stay in the Central Valley. There don't seem to be any square corners or regular windows. Every item has been created individually by hand—no two doors are alike. It's fun, elegant, and small enough to be intimate.

Dinners are prepared and served by advance request only, and are not to be missed. Finca Rosa Blanca is one of only two hotels that have earned the Costa Rican Tourist Board's highest rating for sustainable tourism, five green leaves. They grow their own organic coffee for the enjoyment of guests. *Info: Santa Bárbara de Heredia. www.fincarosablanca.com; Tel. 2269-9392.*

Real Intercontinental Costa Rica $$$$
Located in the suburb of Escazú, this is the nicest of the big-city, full-service hotels in Costa Rica. It is large, modern, luxurious, and has every business convenience expected.

The rooms are extremely comfortable and fully furnished without seeming plush—things are understated in a business-oriented way. Suites and special services floors offer world-class quality. There are several good restaurants with over-the-top buffets. The lobster buffet is legendary, with more than six styles of preparation including the usual grilled, steamed, thermidor, bisque, and on and on. The buffet with a glass of wine or two and coffee runs about $50 per person, but you do get to eat all of the lobster you can honk down.

The pool is huge and there is a fully equipped spa. Meeting rooms are set in the "forest" near the pool and have all the technical amenities needed for a major business conference. *Info: Autopista Próspero Fernandez, San Antonio de Escazú. www.intercontinental.com/SanJose; Tel. 2208-2100, 800/496-7621 US.*

Casa Cristal Boutique Hotel $$$

Also in Escazú, the Casa Cristal is a classy and unique place to stay, full of character and style. There are only seven rooms, and it's quite popular, so you'll need to book well in advance if you're visiting in the high season. There's an expansive view of the city and the mountains, and the property is surrounded by plenty of bird-infested forest. Owners Zeida and Victor are happy to accommodate any special needs, and make the place feel like home.

The rooms range from the surprisingly inexpensive standard suites to the enormous master suite, which features a Jacuzzi, a bidet, a panoramic sliding glass door and a private terrace. All rooms have the full range of mod cons, including AC, free wireless internet, flat-screen TVs, safes, ironing boards and hair dryers. There's a small pool, and spa treatments are on offer.

The Murano restaurant has a splendid view, and the international cuisine is prepared to order by Zeida herself. *Info: Escazú. www.casacristalcr.com; Tel. 2289-2530, 786/206-1506 US.*

Resort Martino $$$

This resort is located across the street from the delightful Zoo Ave just outside Alajuela, convenient to the airport. Operated by an Italian hotelier, it's a friendly, comfortable, well-run establishment. The large and beautifully landscaped grounds are a peaceful oasis.

The 47 modern, spacious rooms and suites have every convenience, including phone, satellite TV, air conditioning and more. The buildings were constructed with imagination, and are filled with exotic woods crafted into unique interiors and furnishings.

There's an enormous pool, gym, spa, conference center and tennis courts. The spa is one of the largest and nicest in the country. The Italian-style restaurant has good food and a nice terrace view. *Info: La Garita de Alajuela. www.hotelmartino.com; Tel. 2433-8382, 888/886-5042 US.*

Alta Hotel $$$
A Mediterranean architectural masterpiece, the Alta is a joy to visit. Stucco, arches and wrought iron fit in perfectly with the verdant tropical landscaping. The lobby and public areas are filled with exhibits of art from local artists. The views are great and it is in a quiet area. It's a bit on the wrong end of town for the international airport, but good for Escazú.

The 23 rooms have all the conveniences expected in a first-class hotel, including internet access, direct-dial phones, minibar, coffee maker, work desk and safe. Tile floors open onto nice balconies or patios, some with panoramic views of the mountains.

The restaurant is one of the most interesting in Costa Rica, specializing in Pacific Rim fusion with local fish and fruit. The wine list and selections at the bar are noble. *Info: West of Escazú on the old road to Santa Ana. www. thealtahotel.com; Tel. 2282-4160, 888/388-2582 US.*

Hampton Inn $$$
This hotel is very close to the airport, and is the usual well-run Hampton Inn like the ones you may have stayed at in the US, with air-conditioning, cable TV, alarm clocks and a passable fruit and cereal breakfast buffet. It's not exactly luxury but it's comfortable, modern and familiar with all the expected in-room goodies.

If you are just changing planes and don't want to go into San José, this is a good spot to stay over. It's about a $12 taxi ride into downtown, and perhaps $2 to the airport. In fact, the airport is close enough that you could walk if you felt like it. *Info: www.hamptoninn.com; Tel. 2436-0000.*

Pura Vida Hotel $$
This is one of my favorites, centrally located in the highlands outside Alajuela about four kilometers from the airport (but out of the flight path) on the route to the coffee growing area and Poás volcano. It's an ideal base for exploring the central valley as well as the whole country.

The owners live on the property and are consummate hosts. They make sure each guest has plenty of tropical fruit smoothies and anything else they need to make their stay memorable. As there are only seven rooms, they can spend lots of time with each guest pampering and advising on travel plans. If you are leaving early in the morning they will arrange transport, wake you up with coffee and provide a nice packed breakfast.

The rooms are all in freestanding casitas, attractively furnished and scattered around nicely landscaped grounds. Heliconias, coffee trees, tomato trees, giant passion fruit and orchids perfume the air. They are pet friendly and have three nice dogs: Yaggi,  Max and Lobo. Yaggi would come by my casita for a visit from time to time when I stayed there.

You should definitely arrange for one of their spectacular dinners served on the patio overlooking the volcano. Nhi and Berni are superb cooks and may just serve you the best meal you will have on your trip.

Guests typically stay their first night or two after flying into the country, then spend their last night there again before catching an early morning flight back home. Because of this travel pattern, the owners are very experienced helping guests coordinate rental cars, hotels and tours and advising on the best things to do and see. They believe that getting from place to place in Costa Rica should be an adventure in itself and not just a transfer in the bowels of a tourist bus. *Info: www.puravidahotel.com; Tel. 2430-2929, 2430-2630.*

Vacation Lodgings

If you plan to stay in one place for a week or more, renting a guest house may be an economical and comfortable alternative to staying at a hotel. Use one of the Costa Rica-based search engines to find a local agent in the region you're interested in (see Web Sites, near the end of the *Practical Matters* chapter). One caveat about renting a place: what you see on a web site and what you find when you arrive may be two different things. Ask plenty of questions, and search online for comments from other travelers who've rented through a particular real estate agent in the past. These sites have links to available rentals in all price ranges, throughout the country:

• *www.viviun.com/Rentals/Costa_Rica*
• *www.goin2travel.com/costa-rica-vacation-rentals.htm*

BEST SLEEPS NORTH OF SAN JOSÉ

Selva Verde Lodge $$

This ecotourism center right on the Sarapiquí River features a small botanical garden and a number of marked trails on the property. Just across the river is primary rain forest. It is waaay out in the jungle. The River Lodge has open rooms on elevated platforms, with nice open wooden verandahs. The newer Bungalow rooms have AC and screened-in balconies. Iguanas hang out by the pool, and you might just see a new bird from the bar or the beautiful porch overlooking the stream. Their nighttime jungle walk might require a couple of cups of coffee first, but is well worth the effort. Hiking, whitewater rafting and serious birding are high on the menu of activities. A complimentary bird watching walk is offered twice a day. *Info: Chilamate, Sarapiquí (about two hours north of San José). www.selvaverde. com; Tel. 2761-1800, 800/451-7111 US.*

BEST EATS IN SAN JOSÉ & THE CENTRAL VALLEY

Here you'll find the country's most cosmopolitan selection of restaurants, from various international cuisines to local specialties, and delightful fusions of the two. Most of the lodges we've recommended have dining.

La Luz $$$$

La Luz is an upscale restaurant in the Alta Hotel in Escazú, with an excellent wine list and an imaginative menu. Seafood, steaks and chicken cooked with **Mediterranean and Asian influences** lead to some interesting combinations likely to upset traditionalists but please the palate. The wine list and bar selection are outstanding. *Info: In the Alta Hotel, west of Escazú on the old road to Santa Ana. www.thealtahotel.com; Tel. 2282-4160.*

Restaurante Grano de Oro $$$

This hotel restaurant has **the best table in San José**. Continental tradition mixed with Costa Rican seafood and produce ensure wonderful tasting, creative dishes. Desserts are singular. The setting is romantic, with potted tropical plants. *Info: Calle 30, Avenidas 2/4. In the Hotel Grano de Oro. www. hotelgranodeoro.com; Tel. 2255-3322.*

El Mirador $$$

El Mirador, atop the Aurola Holiday Inn (see above), cannot be beat for an awesome view over the city. Most of the tables are by the windows that wrap around three sides of the high rise. The atmosphere is piano-tinkling elegant with white shirt, bow tie waiters and a formal but charming Maitre D. The approach is French/continental. I liked the half avocado stuffed with seafood, the beef medallions, and the interesting bread made with rosemary. The wine list is minimal but adequate, with French, Chilean and some good Spanish selections starting around $40. The house wine is a quite acceptable Chilean poured into small glasses at $2 a shot. This is not a problem since the wine steward keeps the glasses full. El Mirador is no more expensive than most of the other nicer restaurants in town, with mains starting around $12. Reservations are recommended. *Info: Calle 5, Avenida 5. www.aurolahotels.com; Tel. 2523-1000.*

Park Café $$$

This little restaurant is in an antique shop in Sabana Norte. The chef has previously run top-rated restaurants in London and in Marrakech, and the food is memorable. *Info: www.parkcafecostarica.blogspot.com; Tel. 2290-6324.*

Restaurant Gourmet La Focaccia $$$

Located in the Hotel Martino just outside Alajuela, Le Gourmet features traditional Italian cuisine utilizing local produce, seafood and steaks, and overlooks the classical pool and gardens. If you hanker for gnocchi, veal or scampi, this is a good choice. It's a little formal but not at all uncomfortable. *Info: La Garita de Alajuela. www.hotelmartino.com; Tel. 2433-8382.*

El Balcón De La Europa $$$

El Balcón is a refreshing break from the usual sea bass, steaks and shrimp dishes served the same old way in most of the upscale Costa Rican restaurants. It offers these standards but with an Italian emphasis. They have a long list of interesting pastas and even risotto. Located just down the street from the infamous Hotel Del Rey, the atmosphere is dark, with black and white drawings and photographs of old Costa Rica along with framed, witty sayings from philosophers and the famous. The prices are a little lower than usual. Try the mixed pasta plate. In spite of the name, there is no balcony. *Info: Calle 9 & Avenida Central. Tel. 2221-4841.*

Vishnu $$

Convenient to downtown, Vishnu is a good spot for a vegetarian health-food meal at almost any time of day. It is a popular place with locals, and you'll see plenty of middle-class, healthy young Ticas scarfing up vegetarian chow. The smoothies are intense. *Info: Avenida 1, near Calle 3. Tel. 2256-6063.*

Marisquería Princesa Marina $$

The Princesa has four locations around San José, including one in Alajuela and one in Escazú. It is a good place to honk down a big pile of shrimp or inexpensive lobster. For under $10 you can gorge on them along with all the usual seafood items. Wine and beer are basic and good. This is one of my favorite places to eat. *Info: Tel. 2232-0481.*

La Casona de Cerdo BBQ & Chicharronera $$

If you turn on the road that goes off in front of the Hampton Inn near the airport towards San José, after about two miles you'll come to a top-quality BBQ emporium complete with a huge stuffed pig in the entry. This is serious pork country, and a popular place with locals. It looks really busy when you drive up but the parking attendants will help you get in and out with little fuss. It's a big place and there is seldom much of a line. *Info: Near Heredia on Rió Segundo Road.*

BEST NIGHTLIFE & ENTERTAINMENT

Because of the unsafe nature of the streets at night, nightlife in San José is perhaps best limited to excursions to the **Jazz Café** in San Pedro, the student part of town. *Info: www.jazzcafecostarica.com; Tel. 2253-8933.*

San José is a world-famous nightlife destination, but most of the fame is based on gambling at the **Horseshoe**, or pursuing the dubious pleasures of ladies of the night at the **Blue Marlin Bar**. *Info: www.delreyhotel.com; Tel. 2257-7800.* Otherwise it would be best to make an early night of it. Get up early and go on a bird walk.

BEST SPORTS & RECREATION
RAFTING

Most **rafting** is done on the **Pacuare** and **Reventazón** rivers, and put-in points for both are easily accessible from the San José area. Outfitters usually arrange for all transportation to and from your hotel, food, etc. You can go on one-day or overnight trips. The Corobici, Sarapiquí, Naranjo and El General rivers are also open for rafters. Two companies dominate the rafting scene and are both quite experienced. **Costa Rica Expeditions** is the oldest and most respected rafting operator. **Ríos Tropicales** is a worthy competitor. *Info: Costa Rica Expeditions: www.costaricaexpeditions. com; Tel. 2257-0766, 2521-6099. Ríos Tropicales: www.riostropicales.com; Tel. 2333-6455, 866/722-8273 US.*

GOLF

Costa Rica has several **championship courses**, all with wonderful tropical foliage, spectacular mountain or ocean vistas, and a bit of jungle wildlife to lend an air of adventure. Operators of golf tours and websites with information on Costa Rican golf include:

• www.costaricagolf.com
• www.teetimescostarica.com
• www.golfcr.com
• www.worldgolf.com/travel/cosrica.html
• www.golfincostarica.com

The country's oldest 18-hole course is at the **Cariari Country Club** near San José, built in the 70s. Unless you have a Costa Rican friend, you won't get to play this beautiful par-71 course, as it's now a private country club. Also in the Central Valley is **Valle del Sol**, a 6,750-yard par-72 course. Designed by Tracy May, it has a uniquely Costa Rican flavor, with fifteen small lakes (watch out for crocodiles), tropical trees and panoramic views of the Irazú, Barva and Poás volcanoes.

5. THE NORTH CARIBBEAN COAST

The northern coastal region is low and jungly, with sleepy rivers and swampy, forested plains fronted by magnificent wild and dangerous sandy beaches. **Hardcore anglers, turtle worshipers and birders indulge their fantasies.** The three villages in the area, Parismina, Tortuguero and Barra del Colorado, offer some of the best wildlife viewing opportunities in the country. You can see monkeys and sloths, crocs and caimans, as well as over 450 bird species, from the comfort of a small boat. The fishing is outstanding.

A labyrinth of canals, marshes, wetlands and rain forest extends for miles and miles inland from the coast, a vast tangle of trees, vines, orchids, fish, birds and monkeys. There are no roads to speak of in this region. You'll arrive here by small plane, and get around by water taxis.

There are three small towns along the coast connected only by small airstrips and inland canals. All have fine lodging, excellent fishing and some of the best wildlife viewing opportunities anywhere.

Parismina is a small village on a spit of land between a slow river and the Atlantic. There are a couple of excellent fishing lodges nearby.

A ride up the canals by launch will take you to **Tortuguero**, a bit larger town also located between a wild beach and a broad river. Nearby is **Tortuguero National Park**, great for trips into the jungle by small boat for wildlife viewing. Bring your camera. Turtles come on to the park beaches at night—don't miss the guided tours. There are several top-quality lodges nearby.

Although there are no lodges dedicated just to fishing in the Tortuguero area, excellent guides are available, and the fishing is probably just as good as in Parismina or Barra del Colorado.

Another launch ride takes you almost to Nicaragua and the village of **Barra del Colorado**. Although the same wildlife-viewing opportunities abound here, the main activity is fishing for enormous tarpon, snook, and a wide variety of jungle fish. Two world-famous fishing lodges are located here.

HIGHLIGHTS

• **Jungle Cruises** – Tortuguero National Park by pontoon boat, great wildlife viewing

• **Luxurious Fishing Lodges** – world-class tarpon and snook fishing in the lagoons, river mouths and offshore

• **Turtle Worship** – nighttime *arribadas* (mass arrivals) of egg-laying leatherbacks

• **Wild Beaches** – beachcomb miles of natural beaches

Actually the entire region is splendid territory for both pursuits—excellent fishing charters are available at all the area lodges. To the north, **Barra del Colorado Wildlife Refuge** is even more remote than Tortuguero National Park and receives far fewer visitors.

COORDINATES
Connected only by canals, the three villages along the 150 miles of coast are not accessible by road—visitors arrive by water taxi or small plane. The wild beaches of the coast run from just north of Limón to the border with Nicaragua.

THE NORTHERN CARIBBEAN IN A DAY
The Caribbean coast is a bit far from San José for day trips, but never fear. You can get in and out of this region in just one day.

Tour operators arrange for small buses to pick up tourists from San José hotels and take them comfortably to the coast to link up with jungle cruises through the canals of **Tortuguero National Park** (see photo below). They somehow manage to bring you back again the same day, exhausted, but just in time for milk and cookies.

Day trips from cruise ships docking at **Limón** usually run launches north up the canals on jungle tours with a stop at a jungle lodge for lunch and then back again in time for shrimp cocktails on board.

If you are staying in one of the lodges in the area, you can arrange for short trips inland on small boats to the rain forest or along coastal canals to gape at wildlife or fish.

A FANTASTIC NORTH CARIBBEAN WEEKEND

A quick overnight or weekend trip to the coast to wrestle with tarpon and snook and visit the rain forest in small boats is quite feasible. Flights from San José to Tortuguero or Barra del Colorado usually run quite early in the morning, so you can easily get in a whole day of fishing or wildlife viewing

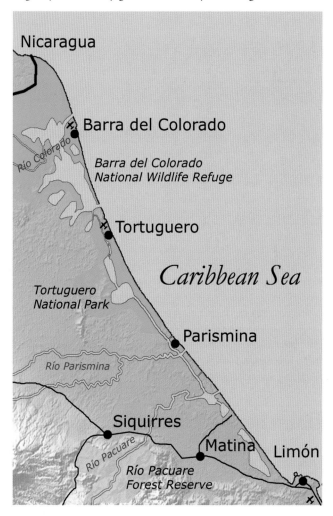

Nicaragua

Barra del Colorado

Río Colorado

Barra del Colorado National Wildlife Refuge

Tortuguero

Caribbean Sea

Tortuguero National Park

Parismina

Río Parismina

Siquirres

Matina Limón

Río Pacuare

Río Pacuare Forest Reserve

on the first day of a weekend trip. Parismina generally takes a bit too long to get to for a short weekend trip.

The lodges around **Tortuguero** are well set up for providing their guests with tours and guides into the rain forest on small boats and for guided walks into Tortuguero National Park for turtle viewing. This is the best area along the coast for wildlife viewing. Most lodges can arrange for top-quality fishing guides, and fishing in the area is excellent for tarpon and snook.

Barra del Colorado has two wonderful, comfortable lodges—both dedicated to fishing for tarpon and snook and to providing their angling clientele with a comfortable setting with buffets groaning with great cooking, plenty of drink and a bar for hanging around in telling lies about how big the fish you caught were. Either can arrange for trips into the rain forest and nearby **Barra del Colorado Wildlife Refuge**.

A weekend enjoying Costa Rica's northern Caribbean coast begins by catching an early half-hour flight out of San José to Barra del Colorado or Tortuguero. Have your camera ready in the plane because, if it's not raining too hard, you can get some good pictures of the lodges, beaches and inlet as the plane makes its approach to the tiny runway.

Barra del Colorado

The lodges in Barra del Colorado are attuned to what **anglers** want: they pick you up planeside, hustle your bags to your room and get you out on the water quickly and comfortably. If you plan your weekend carefully, you can get in two full days of tarpon bashing, and be back in San José Sunday evening ready for *un zarpe*, a nightcap.

There are only a couple of lodges in the area, and they are serious centers of fishing, fishing, and fishing. The people who stay at these lodges spend all day fishing and all night drinking and lying about fishing. People who tease birders for being intense should visit a big-time fishing lodge.

Silver King Lodge and **Río Colorado Lodge** are the choices (see *Best Sleeps* for more details). I have fished many days in both, and I love the lodges, the owners and the people who run them. Both are comfortable, with memorable food, lots of jungle character, top-quality equipment and sharp guides. Their prices are similar. You will probably catch the same amount of fish no matter which lodge you stay at. The success of your fishing trip depends more on luck, time of year, and weather than on where you sleep.

The fishing here is simply spectacular. The fish are large, plentiful and easy to catch. **Tarpon** swarm in their thousands off the river mouths. Offshore, anglers haul in tarpon over 150 pounds on a daily basis, as well as large **jack** and **wahoo**. In the rivers, you'll catch **snook** over 25 pounds, smaller tarpon, **snapper**, **sharks** and exotic local species such as **machaca** and **calba**. If you've a taste for the unusual, you can even catch a **sawfish**.

The lodges are all-inclusive, so you don't have to worry about restaurants or bars. Wine, beer, rum, and in some cases all drinks, are unlimited, and tables groan under enormous dinner buffets. There is little doubt in my mind that some of the best eating in the entire country goes on in the dining rooms of the two lodges in Barra del Colorado.

It's possible to take jungle tours or indulge in spa treatments at most of the lodges, in case for some reason you don't want to spend every available daylight hour fishing.

Snook for Supper

If you love fish, be sure to try **snook**, a delicious light white fish. In the US, snook isn't available at restaurants or markets. In Costa Rica, however, snook are plentiful, and you're certain to see some on the table, especially in the Caribbean region.

Costa Rica's Best Fishing

Costa Rica has so much great fishing it's tough to narrow things down. But for true trip of-a-lifetime fishing, two fisheries stand out: tarpon and snook on the Caribbean, and billfish on the Pacific.

The Barra del Colorado area has monstrous tarpon in the rivers and just offshore, and excellent action for snook and exotic local species in the canals. Take your pick of several excellent lodges.

The Pacific is billfish territory: catches of a dozen sailfish in one day are not unusual. Quepos is the largest sportfishing center in the country, but just about any place on the Pacific can offer a classic fishing trip. Playa Flamingo and Puerto Jiménez are also prime destinations.

Tortuguero

For family members who may not be power anglers, Tortuguero has several lagoon-side lodges such as **Laguna Lodge** and **Tortuga Lodge**, offering comfort and proximity to **Tortuguero National Park**.

A **jungle cruise** in a small boat is one of my favorite ways to get out in the rain forest to view birds, monkeys, crocs, and other interesting wildlife. The canals and creeks around the park are a wonderful place to get very remote, very quickly and comfortably. Kids love it too, and the lodges have pools to keep them busy during umbrella drink hours.

The wild and spectacular beaches of the northern Caribbean side are the nesting grounds of green, leatherback and hawksbill **sea turtles**. The park coordinates carefully controlled nighttime beach walks to see turtles nesting (from a respectful distance). Opportunities to volunteer to help the turtles can be arranged quickly for short or long terms. Contact the **Caribbean Conservation Corporation** to find out more. *Info: www.cccturtle.org; Tel. 352/373-6441 US.*

Tortuguero is also a prime area for tarpon and snook fishing, and is the base of the coast's most famous and respected independent guide, **Captain Eddie Brown**, with his 19-foot center-console, twin Yamaha Bull Shark.

Book well in advance, as he is quite popular. He'll come and pick you up at your lodge and provide everything you need except sunscreen and muscle power for cranking in the over-100-pound tarpon common in the area. *Info: Tel. 8383-6097, 8834-2221.*

1-2 WEEKS ON THE NORTH CARIBBEAN COAST

A week on the Caribbean coast gives you plenty of time to enjoy the beaches, the fishing and the wildlife. With two weeks you can enjoy four very different kinds of vacation experiences, and please all members of the family (or you could simply spend more time pursuing your passion).

With one week, spend three or four days at one of the lodges in the **Barra del Colorado** area: Silver King or Río Colorado (see *Best Sleeps*). Then take a water taxi to **Tortuguero** to stay at one of the canal-side lodges: Laguna Lodge or Tortuga Lodge. Spend the mornings touring nearby Tortuguero National Park by small jungle boat. After lunch, soak in the pool and possibly indulge in a siesta, then have a fine dinner with Concha y Toro Chilean wine and, after dark, take part in turtle worship on the beach.

If you're fortunate enough to have up to two weeks to spend in this region, I suggest the following: Sample the **fishing** at Barra del Colorado and/or Parismina, then spend a few days cruising the jungle and turtle worshipping at Tortuguero, with plenty of time left over for relaxing on the spectacular beaches further down the Caribbean coast.

Tortuguero National Park

One of Costa Rica's most popular national parks, Tortuguero covers 77,000 acres and encompasses no less than eleven different habitats, including several types of rain forests, swamps, and lagoons, each with its own variety of plants and animals. The magnificent 22-mile beach is a favorite **nesting ground** for hawksbill, loggerhead, green and leatherback sea turtles.

There's **no road access** to Tortuguero. You'll arrive by boat from Parismina, or by small plane. Once here, you'll find the park delightfully accessible by small boat and on foot. There is one smallish hill, Cerro Tortuguero, but no mountains to stress hikers walking in the rain forest. Photographers and birders are especially drawn to the area since wildlife is relatively easy to get close to in the narrow, covered jungle tour boats.

For me, tours through the jungle by boat are the very best way to see wildlife and enjoy the tropical rain forest. Hiking up and down mountains through the cloud forest is fine for some people, but I'll take sitting back in a small boat drifting through backwater creeks. Some of my best wildlife photography has been done on a jungle cruise in Tortuguero. Transportation and tours to the park are best arranged through your lodge (see *Best Sleeps*).

Tortuguero is famous for the **hawksbill, loggerhead, green** and **leatherback sea turtles** that come here to lay their eggs on the beach. In fact, the name of the park refers to a turtle hunter. In years past, tortugueros hunted the green turtle almost to extinction, not only for meat but also for the supposed aphrodisiac qualities of their eggs.

In 1959, Dr. Archie Carr of the University of Florida founded a local organization to preserve sea turtles. Today, the turtles' reproductive rites take place under our paternal gaze: no one is allowed on the beach unaccompanied at night, prime laying time, so you'll have to arrange for a guide (which you can do through your lodge) to watch mama turtle dig her nest in the sand or, if you are very lucky, to see the hatchlings scurry to the sea. Hawksbill, loggerhead, and Pacific green turtles nest from July through October. The leatherback, the world's largest sea turtle, nests from February through July. Learn more about Costa Rica's sea turtles at *www.costaricaturtles.com* and *www.cccturtle.org*.

Inland from the beaches lies a labyrinth of freshwater canals and lagoons, inhabited by manatees, river otters, caimans, turtles, and over 50 species of freshwater fish, to say nothing of the monkeys, sloths and birds you'll see on the banks. There are three park stations, all open 8am-4pm. **Cuatro Esquinas Headquarters** is in the town of Tortuguero, and features trails along the beaches. Camping is available. The **Sector Jalova Station** is further south, near Jalova Lagoon and the town of Parismina. On the western border of the park, **Aguas Frías Station** has a trail that leads to the highest point in the park at Lomas del Sierpe (1,000 feet). *Info: Entry to the park is $10 for adults. Tel. 2709-8086.*

Barra del Colorado National Wildlife Refuge

North of Tortuguero, along the border with Nicaragua, **Barra del Colorado National Wildlife Refuge** is even larger (at 200,000 acres, Costa Rica's second-largest rain forest preserve) and more remote. Like Tortuguero, most of the park is a maze of canals, creeks, sloughs, bayous and every sort of watery landscape, inhabited by crocs, caimans, manatees and the usual vast array of animals and birds.

Here you can get nose-to-nose with critters, with none of the crowds further south in Tortuguero. The refuge is accessible only by boat, so you'll need to arrange a tour through your lodge.

Don't Feed the Monkeys

Everyone loves monkeys, and in Costa Rica, you can get a close-up look at their antics. They're rowdy little characters, however, so use caution. At remote lodges, the precocious primates may waltz right in through an open window and help themselves to food or unguarded belongings. When monkeys are encouraged by tourists feeding them, they can get aggressive and may even bite. Watch your belongings, **don't try to pet them**, and whatever you do, **do not feed them**. Standing directly under monkeys in trees is also not recommended.

Barra del Colorado village is a cluster of run-down shacks with a colorful history that includes Nicaraguan refugees and gun and drug smugglers. Today it has few facilities other than the airstrip, and is of no particular interest to tourists. *Info: Entrance to the refuge costs $6 per person, which you pay at the ranger station near the Silver King Lodge. There are no tourist facilities to speak of, but information is available at Diana's Souvenirs in the village of Barra del Colorado.*

North Caribbean Beaches

Beaches north of Limón are **wild, remote and dangerous**. Huge piles of driftwood stretch into the distance for miles. The surf is thunderous with heavy undertow. **Bull sharks** feed among the breakers. There are no beachfront restaurants or other facilities, except at a few of the Tortuguero-area lodges. If you are a serious beach hiker you will love the north Caribbean beaches. If you are a regular old beach lover, then head for the beaches south of Limón, where you'll find safe swimming spots and plenty of places to get a cold beer.

BEST SLEEPS & EATS
The two regions of the Caribbean coast (north or south of Limón) are quite different, primarily because there are roads in the south, but the only travel in the north is by boat or small plane. Consequently, almost all of the tourist facilities in the north are planned around all-inclusive lodges, with little of interest going on in the small villages. **Dining in at your all-inclusive lodge is really the only option**. Most lodges serve huge buffets with excellent resort cuisine and plenty to choose from.

BEST SLEEPS IN PARISMINA
There is not much reason to come to Parismina except for fishing, but that's more than enough to draw thousands of visitors each year from all over the world to this remote little village. The tarpon and snook fishing are world-class, and Tortuguero National Park begins just north of the inlet. The **Tortuguero Canal**, the main means of travel in the north Caribbean, runs right through "town." Guides are available for organized turtle worship on the beaches at night when they come ashore to lay eggs.

Río Parismina Lodge $$$
Judy Heidt has been running what is arguably the most famous fishing lodge in Costa Rica for more than 20 years. The rooms are comfortable (free laundry service), the food outstanding and the fishing fleet one of

the best on the coast. Most of her guides have been with her for at least a decade. You can get to the lodge from San José by bus and boat, if flying to isolated runways in small planes isn't your thing.

This is a serious fishing lodge, but there is still plenty to do for non-fishing guests. All the usual tours are available, with turtle worship at the nearby Tortuguero National Park a specialty. Few people come to this end of the park to visit, so you avoid the crowds. There is a nice pool and Jacuzzi.

Coffee is brought right to your door every morning at 5am, and a lavish breakfast buffet with freshly baked pastries and piles of tropical fruits is presented. If you move quickly, you can be fighting a tarpon by 6am. After fishing, the booze flows as freely as you like, accompanied by delicious bocas and the usual fishy conversation. Judy is a superb hostess and holds several world records herself.

Expect to fish more with live bait and circle hooks than with lures. **Snook fishing** at the mouth of the inlet is done both by slow trolling and casting from the shore. I admit I've never personally caught anything surf fishing here, but enthusiasts swear the biggest snook are caught this way. *Info: www.riop.com; Tel. 800/338-5688 US.*

BEST SLEEPS IN TORTUGUERO

Tortuguero is all about turtles, jungle cruises and hikes through Tortuguero National Park. Lodges line the canal near the airport and the charmingly tiny and not-quite-grubby village. **Tortuga Lodge** (see photo below) is the best. **Manatus**, **Laguna** and **Mawamba** are also very nice.

The village itself has a couple of small backpacker lodgings and a couple of *sodas* where you can arrange for seafood dinners at reasonable prices. Some small tour operators have offices in the village. There is quite a nice gift shop by the main dock. You can see the gigantic plastic toucan in front from far away, announcing the type of things on offer inside.

BEST OF THE BEST –
OUR FAVORITE LODGING IN THE
NORTH CARIBBEAN
Tortuga Lodge $$$

This is the nicest lodge in the area. It's conveniently located across from the airstrip (don't worry about noise, this isn't O'Hare - just a few propellor planes per day). The rooms are in a two-story motel-style building, and have hammocks and ceiling fans, as well as sizable, comfortable beds and stylish tile bathrooms with hair dryers. There are no TVs or phones, but there is free wireless internet. All the rooms overlook the river, but the upstairs ones are nicer (and slightly more expensive), as they get more breeze, and feature balconies with better views.

The food leans toward local seafood and is served communally on long tables in a screened-in room overlooking the river, a peaceful place to compare notes with other travelers. The pool is small but refreshing after a long day visiting the nearby park or fishing.

Tortuga Lodge is operated by **Costa Rica Expeditions**, and they run a tight, well-managed ship. Guides and tours can be arranged through the lodge, and utilize the lodge's own dedicated guides, who are trained and certified by Costa Rica Expeditions.

Although not primarily a fishing destination, Tortuguero has tarpon and snook fishing just about as good as you can find anywhere. Guides such as world-famous **Captain Eddie Brown** operate from the lodge and can take you for an unforgettable angling experience. *Info: www.tortugalodge.com; Tel. 2257-0766, 2521-6099.*

Manatus Hotel $$$

Everybody loves this small and cheerful lodge. The 12 rooms are not exactly luxurious (nor are any others in this part of the country) but are stylish and comfortable, with AC, TV, spotless bathrooms and outdoor showers. The small pool is  right by the river. There's a small fitness room and a computer center with internet access. Massages and a variety of spa treatments can be scheduled in your room.

The open-air restaurant has a view of the water and a menu with the usual seafood and local/international favorites.

Packages include meals and a jungle cruise per day, but - unlike many local lodges - not drinks. There's a resident sloth or two, and the usual howler monkeys and birds perform their tropical serenade. This isn't a hard-core fishing lodge, but world-class fishing trips can of course be arranged. Honeymoon packages are also popular. *Info: www.manatuscostarica.com; Tel. 2239-4854, 2709-8197.*

Laguna Lodge $$$

On the beach side of the canal, Laguna is aimed mostly at large groups of **package tourists** being herded from San José or from cruise ships docking in nearby Limón. The flower-filled grounds and pool are beautiful, and they have well-organized tours of all types. The rooms are air-conditioned, with safes and the usual amenities. There are no TVs in the rooms—no problem for me. The beach is wild and sandy with lots of driftwood, not

 suitable for swimming but great for walks. The lodge is well managed and comfortable. Manager Yury runs a tight ship and everything is spotless. The main buildings, restaurant and bar are built in a wild, Gaudiesque style with freeform railings and

soaring rooflines. Live entertainment in the bar before dinner is quite touristy, often resulting in spontaneous conga lines sashaying into the buffet.

Guests are divided up into groups of 10 or so and encouraged to eat together, and are assigned to the same guides for the duration of their stay. This way you get to make friends and get to know the guides a bit. Call for specials. *Info: www.lagunatortuguero.com; Tel. 2272-4943, 888/259-5615 US.*

Mawamba Lodge $$$

Also on the beach side, Mawamba exudes **tropical ambiance**. The large and extravagant pool ensures kids will have plenty to do. This is a good

base for exploring the nearby park in small boats and turtle worship on the beach. Like the Laguna Lodge, it is in between the river and the dramatic beach. Walks on the Tortuguero beach are spectacular, but it's way too rough for safe swimming. Most guests are on package deals that include tours and meals.

The jungle cruises up and down the river are famous. Buffets are the usual tourist fare with tropical fruits and local specialties. The same company operates the wonderful Trogon Lodge near Cerro de La Muerte. *Info: www.grupomawamba.com; Tel. 2293-8181.*

BEST SLEEPS IN BARRA DEL COLORADO

Barra del Colorado consists of two shabby villages on either side of the river near the inlet, and two wonderful fishing lodges. There is no action here whatsoever except for fishing and exploring the nearby park. The beaches are wild and rough. The inlet is well known for being home to bull sharks and crocodiles as well as huge tarpon and snook.

The two lodges below differ slightly in their prices and services—but not much. Both are wonderful places to stay, and you are just about as likely to catch loads of fish at one as at the others. Both are quite comfortable, and dripping with tropical fishing lodge charm.

The food at these lodges is legendary. These are some of the best places to eat in the entire country.

The anglers, who come from all over the world for the unique fishing, are paying huge amounts of money for the privilege, and tend to be high-earning executives, trust fund babies and wealthy entertainers accustomed to wining and dining in the finest restaurants of the world. They expect similar cuisine when they fish.

These lodges supply both the world-class cuisine and the world-class tarpon and snook. Any of the lodges in the area will arrange your entire trip from the time you leave home until you arrive, ready to fish. This is a good option, as the only way to get here is by small plane and boat.

Silver King Lodge $$$

Silver King has not only the best boats and guides but also the nicest rooms and pool in the area. The rooms are large, spotlessly clean and air-conditioned, with nice furniture and coffee makers. Internet access is available for guests. **Their food is some of the best I've eaten anywhere in Costa Rica**. The groaning morning, noon and evening buffets are filled with dozens of meats, fish and gourmet specialties better than a dozen grandmas or French chefs could make.

The service is really special. As you step off your boat every evening you are handed an amazing frozen tropical cocktail and directed to the pool and Jacuzzi, where snacks and more drinks await. Any clothes you drop on the floor are washed and placed back in your room daily. Every night before bedtime, there is a tap at the door and you are presented with an insulated pitcher of ice water.

The lodge makes its own boats and uses top-quality gear. The boats are well outfitted with all the modern fishing electronics as seen on TV. Even more important, the local guides know how to put you onto the fish.

Fanatical anglers who buy fishing magazines and watch the fishing shows on Saturday morning TV know that the Caribbean side of Costa Rica offers the world's top tarpon and snook fishing. Tarpon over 100 pounds school up in thousands off the river mouths and over sandy bottoms off-shore. Snook over 20 pounds are caught surf fishing near the river mouths or by trolling and casting in lagoons. The Silver King Lodge is where those fishing fanatics would like to be right now.

A unique offering is a specially designed "photo boat" that follows anglers as they fish with a professional photographer who captures your exploits on digital camera. The photos are downloaded to personalized CDs and provided to you at the end of your stay at no additional charge. *Info: www. silverkinglodge.net; Tel. 877/335-0755 US.*

Río Colorado Lodge $$$

An old Mississippi charmer, Dan Wise is a genial host, and tells some of the most preposterous, but perhaps true, fishing stories you'll hear any-where. The lodge is old and funky but comfortable and full of character. The rooms are well appointed, with individual air conditioning, good reading lights and hot water.

The food tends toward down-home Southern specialties with plenty of seafood and Dan's grandmother's fried chicken recipe. Equipment is top-notch and the guides very experienced. This lodge is the closest one to the ac-tion. Many record-breaking fish have been caught here, including a world-record machaca, landed from their dock using a banana for bait.

Hanging around the dock and bar at Río Colorado for conversation and lies after fishing all day is one of life's great pleasures. This is one of my favorite places to stay in the world. Río Colorado's package deals are hard to beat. *Info: www.riocoloradolodge.com; Tel. 2232-4063, 2232-8610, 800/243-9777 US.*

Bountiful Buffets

The **all-inclusive fishing lodges** in the north, such as Silver King, Rió Parismina Lodge and Rió Colorado, offer groaning buffets of down-home and tropical cooking ten grandmas couldn't duplicate. The fresh fish, **snook and snapper**, will always be a star on those tables. The dessert buffets are dangerous.

BEST NIGHTLIFE & ENTERTAINMENT

Although you can find some action in the cantinas in the villages, you will probably be well-ensconced in your lodge by nightfall and may do well to hang around in your resort bar. Most have nice views over the river. I always enjoy mixing with congenial fellow travelers, and these lodges are good places to meet people for a chat.

BEST SPORTS & RECREATION
BIRDING

The northern Atlantic coastal area is low, with a long sandy beach coast-line paralleled by the inland waterway and black water swamps. Well **over 450 bird species** have been observed in the area including many endemic species (crimson-fronted parakeet, rufous-winged woodpecker, and bare-necked umbrella bird). There are not as many water birds as you might expect and much of the mangrove areas have been converted for farming.

The area is not on the most common birding itineraries but serious twitchers will love the variety and ease of observation.

This is the habitat for green ibis, spoonbills, rufescent tiger-herons, green and rufous kingfishers, tinamous, and, of course, various parrots. If lucky, you may see a Montezuma oropendula or a limpkin.

Top tour agency Costa Rica Expeditions has, by far, the best-trained guides in the country—several are top bird guides. Count yourself lucky indeed if you can get Carlos Gomez—probably the top bird guide in the country. Their lodge in Tortuguero would be my choice for a base for birding activities up and down the coast.

FISHING
The northern Caribbean region of Costa Rica is a world-class fishing destination for tarpon and snook. You pretty much have to stay in one of the all-inclusive fishing lodges to bag one of these coveted game fish. Fishing lodges in this area are some of the best in the country. You could let Costa Rica Outdoors handle the whole thing: they specialize in fishing packages.

Info: *www.costaricaoutdoors.com; Tel. 2231-0306, 2231-0673 or 800/308-3394 US.*

The lodges on the Caribbean side are clustered around **Parismina** and **Barra del Colorado**. You can only get to them by boat or small plane. None of them are in the category of "luxury" but they are all comfortable, with AC and wonderful food. Your chances of catching fish are about the same at any of them. All are steeped in character. See *Best Sleeps & Eats*, above, for information on the local lodges.

6. THE SOUTH CARIBBEAN COAST

The southern part of Costa Rica's Caribbean coast is famous for a **laid-back atmosphere** and a little "Rasta" flavor. Hard-core fishing fans and wildlife enthusiasts tend to visit the northern Caribbean, whereas the travelers who come down south are more interested in beaches, partying, snorkeling and surfing. You'll find spectacular beaches backed by mountains and rain forest. The flavor is very Caribbean, with some locals speaking a Creole dialect of English and sporting dreadlocks. Surfing, snorkeling and hanging out on the beach are the main activities.

Spend some time chilling out at one of the Rasta-flavored beach towns south of Limón, such as **Puerto Viejo** or **Manzanillo**. Steer clear of Limón itself, a dirty and noisy port city of little interest. Explore the natural wonders of **Cahuita National Park**, both above and below the water. If time permits, visit the remote **Gandoca-Manzanillo National Wildlife Refuge**.

In this part of Costa Rica, Latin culture mixes with a more Caribbean vibe. Many of the locals are black folks who speak a Creole dialect of English, and cook in a more Caribbean style. Occasionally there is the smell of herb.

The beaches are astoundingly pretty, with coconut palms, clear water and coral reefs. Surfing the **Salsa Brava** is a dream for hardcore **surfers. Cahuita** and **Puerto Viejo** are the spots for **diving** and **snorkeling**. Both these towns have plenty of tourist activities, laid-back bars, interesting restaurants with Caribbean spices and dance clubs for the energetic. Alternative youth culture festers in surfer enclaves.

Remember, most of Costa Rica's urban centers, including San José, Limón and Liberia, are generally dirty, noisy, choked with traffic, and not very safe places. Despite what other guidebooks may say, there is very little of interest in any of the cities, unless you're really interested in decayed colonial architecture or sleazy bar culture.

HIGHLIGHTS

• **Cool Caribbean Beaches** – Surfing, dudes!

• **Manzanillo** – end-of-the-road ambiance

• **Rasta-flavored beach villages**

You'll find better lodgings, better restaurants and a generally more relaxed and pleasant atmosphere, at jungle lodges and beach resorts outside of towns. And, after all, it's the jungles and beaches you're going to Costa Rica for, so why not spend your time close to the action?

COORDINATES
The Caribbean coast runs southeast from grimy Limón past multi-colored sand beaches to Cahuita, through funky Puerto Viejo to even funkier Manzanillo. From there it's a 10-mile walk to the border with Panama.

ONE GREAT DAY ON THE SOUTH CARIBBEAN COAST
The south Caribbean coast is too far for a day trip from San José. Day trips from cruise ships docking at Limón usually run launches or arrange for shuttle vans to take passengers to nearby nature preserves and beaches then back to the ship again in time for nachos and bean dip on board.

Morning
The **Sloth Sanctuary** makes a nice day trip. It's easy to visit in the morning, leaving the afternoon for lounging about on the beach.

This privately-run wildlife refuge (formerly known as Aviarios del Caribe) is on the coast just north of Cahuita, where the Estrella River meets the

sea. Since 1991, Americans Judy and Luis Arroyo have made it their mission to rescue and rehabilitate sloths with special needs, and to study the behavior of Costa Rica's two species of sloths. You can visit the famous Buttercup and the other residents at the rehabilitation center, and learn more about these gentle creatures (this is a great place to bring the kids).

If you'd like to see sloths in their natural habitat, you can take a boat tour in the freshwater canals that wind through the wildlife sanctuary. You'll probably also see caimans, turtles, *Pizotes*, and monkeys. The fortunate may be entertained by the antics of river otters or kinkajous. Over 300 bird species have been catalogued. There's also a nice easy walking trail. The lodge has six rooms with private bath that start around $100 double (including breakfast). *Info: Just off the main coast road about 31 km south of Limón. The entrance is about half a mile before you get to the bridge over the Río Estrella. Boat tours are offered from 7am to 2:30pm Tue-Sun for $25 per person ($15 for kids ages 5-11). Closed Mondays. www.slothsanctuary.com; Tel. 2750-0775.*

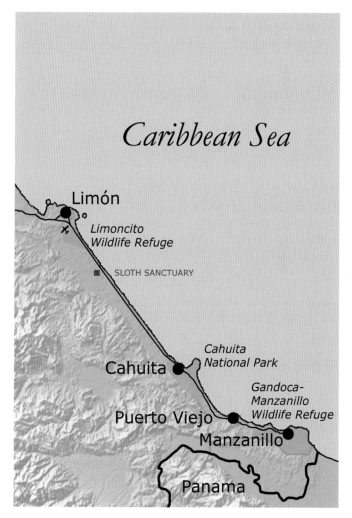

Afternoon
The road south from Limón passes by dozens and dozens of **beaches**. Most are sandy with areas of coral and rock with palm trees and other tropical vegetation. Each beach has its own sand color from almost white through yellow and brown to iridescent black. Very cool!

Depending on your transportation, you can stop off at several beaches on your way back from the Sloth Sanctuary. There are also several cool beaches south towards Cahuita.

Most of the beaches in this area feature **rough surf and plenty of undertow** but are great for long walks and careful swimming.

A FANTASTIC WEEKEND ON THE SOUTH CARIBBEAN COAST

This region is eminently doable as a weekend trip, but it is a good idea to use a tour company: they can make arrangements to fly you to the small airstrip south of Limón, then arrange for a van to the interesting areas of the south coast. Heading down here on your own would mean either a fairly long drive from San José or a hassle finding ground transportation (the Limón airstrip has no car rental facilities), making it impractical for a two or three-day trip. Some lodges will arrange for an airport pick up/drop off.

Friday Evening

Unlike Costa Rica's Pacific coast, the southern Caribbean coast has nothing that you could really call a luxury resort, but there are plenty of modest but comfortable bed-and breakfast-style lodgings in the area around Cahuita and Puerto Viejo, several near gorgeous beaches.

Choose a hotel close to the beach, like **Azania Bungalows** on Playa Cocles, and surrender yourself to the laid-back tropical lifestyle.

Costa Rica's Creoles

The area south of Limón is home to an ethnic group quite different from the Spanish-speaking Mestizos. These black **Creoles** are descendants of Jamaicans who immigrated here in the 19th century to work on banana plantations. They speak a dialect of English similar to the Patois spoken in Jamaica, and **cultural ties to the Anglophone Caribbean are strong**. You'll notice a difference not only in the local language, but also in the cuisine, the music and the general lifestyle. Cool breeze, mon!

There are several great restaurants where local seafood is superb. Of particular note is **La Pecora Nera**, southeast of Puerto Viejo, for an Italian angle on things with fresh, fresh, fresh fish. The ultimate end-of-the-road beach bar is **Maxi's** at the end of the road in Manzanillo. Sit upstairs to check out the beach action while sipping an Imperial. Try the whole snapper (*pargo entero*).

If nightlife is your thing, or a big part of your thing, then select lodging near either Cahuita or Puerto Viejo. It's not a good idea to walk more than a short distance at night, so be sure you have your transportation sorted before you set out.

Saturday

Rise late in the morning and savor a cup of some of the finest coffee in the world. Spend the day lazily strolling along the beach, or pay a visit to **Cahuita National Park**.

From Cahuita all the way down to Manzanillo, huge rocks and stands of coral punctuate endless expanses of gray and black sand. Coconut palms droop gracefully, shading funky little beach bars where locals and tourists go to seed at their own pace. The water is usually quite clear and Caribbean blue, but the surf is dangerous in places. You can snorkel, fish, surf or just drink.

Even if you've never been scuba diving or snorkeled before, you really must rent some snorkeling gear and have a look at the easily accessible reefs. The undersea world of a tropical coral reef is simply too beautiful to miss (and it may not be around forever).

The forests are home to a splendid variety of animals, including howler and capuchin monkeys, sloths and the ubiquitous *Pizotes*, as well as all sorts of aquatic and jungle birds. *Info: There are two access points to Cahuita National Park: Kelly Creek Ranger Station, just south of the village of Cahuita, Tel. 2755-0461; and Puerto Vargas Ranger Station, 3 km further south, Tel. 2755-0302. Entrance costs $10.*

In the evening find your way into Puerto Viejo to mingle with the international youth scene. Drink a little rum and listen to some Reggae music.

Sunday

Wake up early and stroll the beach near your hotel or take a ride south to the end of the road at Manzanillo and walk the trail through the old cacao plantations to secret beaches known only to surfers and their acolytes. Have a memorable seafood lunch at Maxi's before heading back to wherever you came from—relaxed and recharged.

A WEEK ON THE SOUTH CARIBBEAN COAST

Hardcore **beach bums and surfers** would absolutely love a week or two in this laid-back region. More typical tourists, especially those with kids in tow, may start to get bored after a week, as the area doesn't have quite the wealth of touristy activities that you'll find around Manuel Antonio or Monteverde. If you want to get deep into the tropical forest, then a week or two is almost mandatory, as **the best wildlife refuges in the region are quite remote.**

South From Limón

Skip Limón if at all possible. In spite of recent efforts to pretty things up for cruise ship visitors, it is a run-down, rough port town, unpleasant and hot.

Fortunately there is a turnoff to the south at the edge of town, so you can drive right by and not bother with it at all. South of Limón, the beaches are mostly black or gray sand with big rocks and coconut palms backed by mountains and dense rain forest. While the north is only accessible by small plane or boat (part of its charm), the south is tourist-friendly, with a reasonably well-paved road running from Limón to just past **Manzanillo**.

If you are seriously interested in tropical ecology, or would just like to have a close-up look at mountainous rain forest, then don't miss **Selva**

Bananito Lodge. The lodge is right at the edge of the largest protected area in all of Latin America: **Parque International La Amistad**, a vast and diverse biosphere with thousands of acres of undisturbed forest. Arrange transportation with the lodge, as they are somewhat remote. Naturalists and birders flock here to enjoy unspoiled, primary forest.

Around Cahuita

Cahuita National Park features 8.5 miles of beaches backed by rivers, swamps and rain forest, as well as one of Costa Rica's few stretches of coral reef (sadly degraded from agricultural runoff and earthquake upheaval but still nice). At the beaches sheltered by the offshore reef, the water is calm and safe for swimming.

You can **snorkel** out to the reef, which is to the north off Puerto Vargas, but for serious diving action, hire a guide and boat in Cahuita village. In addition to the usual Caribbean profusion of brightly colored coral and fish, there are two small shipwrecks in about 30 feet of water.

Around Manzanillo

The remote **Gandoca-Manzanillo National Wildlife Refuge** near the Panamanian border sees few visitors. It features yet another spectacular beach, rain forests, mangrove swamps and a bit of coral reef. The lagoon is a nursery for tarpon, snook, dorado and tiny billfish. Local fishermen have secret tarpon fishing spots near the border.

Leatherback sea turtles use this area for their nesting grounds, but there is no organized turtle worship as practiced in Tortuguero. If you encounter turtles involved in their nesting routine, you should keep 20 to 30 feet away and turn off all lights. Other aquatic animals include caimans, crocodiles, manatees and a rare species of dolphin called the *tucuxi*.

The beach here is absolutely magnificent, but the pounding surf makes it **unsafe for swimming**. Gandoca, near the south end of the park, can be reached (at least in the dry season) by a tiny and terrible dirt road. There is said to be bus service. Manzanillo, on the coast in the middle of the park, has a few budget lodgings. You can also tour the park by boat from Cahuita.

The area around Manzanillo is known as a destination for *gringas* from North America and Europe who come for a romantic fling with a willing local.

BEST SLEEPS & EATS
BEST SLEEPS NEAR CAHUITA
Selva Bananito Lodge $$
Located adjacent to **Parque International La Amistad**, Selva Bananito is one of the best places to learn about tropical ecology. This re-

mote lodge was established at the edge of a cattle ranch run on low-impact principles, with **more than 2,000 acres left undisturbed**. Primary rain forest is one of the main draws for scientists and serious birders.

The accommodations are basic, but no one comes here for luxury. The proximity to unspoiled forest draws guests looking for outdoor activities and the opportunity to see an outstanding variety of wildlife, including **over 300 species of birds**. Ornithologists are on staff for consultation. *Info: www.selvabananito.com; Tel. 2253-8118.*

BEST SLEEPS NEAR PUERTO VIEJO
Funky, rustic and laid-back are some of the (kinder) adjectives applied to this little oceanfront village. It features beautiful beaches, a bit of coral reef for snorkeling, and a colorful party scene. This area tends to attract surfers, backpackers and the granola set, rather than luxury travelers.

Azania Bungalows $$
Just south of Puerto Viejo, Azania is extremely nice for the price. It's right across the street from **Playa Cocles**, a beautiful expanse of white sand and shady palm trees. It's an excellent surfing beach (the local nickname is

"beach break"), but it also has calm areas that are good for swimming (and—a rarity—occasionally a lifeguard on duty).

The rooms are in typically tropical bungalows with a deck and hammock. Each has two large beds and groovy, almost outdoors yet private bathrooms, ceiling fans and mosquito nets, but no AC. Wi-fi works reasonably well. They have a nice free form pool and Jacuzzi. The restaurant, with an Argentinean chef, and the bar are quite good enough to keep you from wandering into town. *Info: Just south of Puerto Viejo. www.azania-costarica.com; Tel. 2750-0540.*

Villas del Caribe $$

For the price, this is also a great choice. The villas, which sleep up to six people, have balconies and ceiling fans, and some have AC. There are also some two-level villas with all the goodies, including kitchens. They front right on the beach and some sleep up to eight people. There are dozens of palm trees dotted about and the beach is only a few feet away from the rooms. Puerto Viejo is a short bike ride away and there are a couple of small bars and such reasonably close by. The place is a little older and run-down but it still has charm. Avoid the restaurant if possible. *Info: www.villasdelcaribe.com; Tel. 2233-2200.*

Skip Almonds and Corals

The glossy brochures and website make **Almonds and Corals** in the Gandoca Manzanillo Wildlife Refuge look like a tropical honeymoon paradise, but the reality is anything but. The tents are on platforms over a swamp, with little privacy and lots of mosquitoes. Stinkpots emitting black smoke line the walkways at night to keep mosquitoes more or less at bay. There are no safes in the rooms, and we have observed that the safe at the front desk has been left open all day (and perhaps all night) as dozens of employees and others bustle around. Perhaps this is no longer the case but still, why take the chance? There is a tacky and simple zip line on the grounds. There are many nicer places to stay nearby.

Cashew Hill Jungle Lodge $
This laid-back little lodge is up on a hill above Puerto Viejo, with a splendid view of Salsa Brava and Cahuita Bay. Friendly owners Erich & Wendy Strebe bought the place in 2003 and have made several improvements. There are seven cottages with full kitchen facilities and free wi-fi. Groups of up to 18 people can rent the entire lodge. Yoga and massage are on offer, and there's a dog and a cat. *Info: www.cashewhill-lodge.co.cr; Tel. 2750-0256.*

BEST EATS ON THE SOUTH CARIBBEAN COAST

South of Limón you can find funky local eateries with spicy, Caribbean-influenced food, as well as innovative tourist-oriented places with wonderful fresh seafood. It's a little hard to find really cheap eats. The tourist places are usually quite good but the prices may seem a little over the top. Cahuita and Puerto Viejo both have a couple of happening hot spots for spicy local specialties.

A growing tourist trade has spawned a crop of trendy places to try out interesting tropical/new-world fusions and a few especially interesting local joints remain and even improve. Fine dining has found its way to the the south Caribbean coast of Costa Rica, to star alongside the Tico and Jamaican flavors already there. Seafood is almost always going to be a good thing to order.

La Pecora Nera $$$
This Italian restaurant serves up wonderful seafood, and happens to be **the best restaurant on the whole south Caribbean coast**. Don't miss a meal here. Be sure to ask for specials. Lunch is always an option if things are crowded in the evening. Reserva-

Turtles, Not Luxury
Don't expect luxury, but do expect comfortable lodging convenient to beaches and outdoor attractions. Turtles and monkeys are the draw in the north, rather than discos and drinking. The south has more variety, and some people come specifically to enjoy the social aspects of the **youth culture of surfing and fun** that thrives in the area.

tions are essential. When I stopped in for lunch one time, a local fisherman came into the restaurant with several huge snapper for sale. He left
with a grin and a wad of banknotes in his pocket as the cook carried the
fish into the back. The daily special suddenly became snapper. Delicious.
Info: South of Puerto Viejo. Tel. 2750-0490.

Sobre las Olas $$$

Everybody loves this beachfront seafood restaurant. The fishy menu is
livened up by a few Italianesque dishes such as swordfish carpaccio and
tiramisu. If you were any closer to the ocean, your feet would get wet. *Info:
By Playa Negra in Cahuita.*

Maxi's $$

Almost at the end of the road in Manzanillo, a fishing village of just a few
small houses, is Maxi's, a soulful restaurant that serves fresh **fish, shrimp
and lobster**. This is the center of the (small) local scene. I like to grab a
seat that overlooks the beach to sip beer, enjoy some people watching and
eat a *pargo entero* (whole red snapper). This would be a good place to go to
seed. *Info: You can't miss it.*

Miss Edith's $$

This is the best place in the area for a delicious authentic Caribbean meal.
Your stomach needs to be up to the strong Caribbean flavors, though. Be
prepared for spicy food. If you order fish you might get just that, with
head, bones, and all. Edith's is the most interesting place to eat on the
south coast, and the namesake cook, who declares that "love is the most
important ingredient," one of the most interesting people to meet. You
have to stop here at least once. Typical of Jamaican restaurants, the service
is excruciatingly slow. "Soon come." *Info: Cahuita. Tel. 2755-0248.*

BEST NIGHTLIFE

Most of the cool nightlife on the south coast is found in Puerto Viejo
rather than in Cahuita. Manzanillo has Maxi's. That's it but it's enough.

Puerto Viejo is pretty small and you can walk from club to bar to restaurant and back to your lodgings. There are a couple of standards you
will have to at least check out briefly, even if you don't stay all night. Try
Johnny's Place but don't look for Bamboo; it burned to the ground. **Bar
Maritza** hosts mostly locals on Sunday nights and usually has good *salsa*
(music). **Café Viejo** is a little more sophisticated, as it were, with music
ranging through electronic house and trance style.

BEST SPORTS & RECREATION
DIVING
There are a few dive operators in Cahuita, Puerto Viejo and Manzanillo. The better reefs are to the south but although nice and well worth diving, none of the reefs on Costa Rica's Caribbean are in the same class as the ones in nearby Honduras, Cuba or the Caymans.

Reef Runners is a full-service PADI dive shop in Puerto Viejo. *Info: Tel. 2750-0480.*

Aquamor Talamanca Adventure does two-tank boat dives out of Manzanillo for a mere $59. *Info: www.greencoast.com/aquamor.htm. Tel. 2759-9012.*

FISHING
There is not a well-developed sport fishing business in the area but you can certainly find local fishermen to take you out in *pangas* for snapper, jack and perhaps a wahoo.

There are a few tarpon hot spots in the south. I hear rumors of huge tarpon lurking in the hard-to-get-to Laguna Gandoca near the border with Panama. However, the north coast is only a few miles away and is considered perhaps the best place in the world to pursue the silver king.

BIRDING
There are several excellent birding trails you can get to on your own. There is also the birders' dream destination: **Selva Bananito Lodge**. If you stay there you are guaranteed to add significantly to your life list.

Expect to see a wide variety of birds, as there are several quite distinct environments in the area ranging from mangrove swamps to mountain slopes to dense, humid rain forest. Look for such interesting specimens as the rufous motmot, white ringed flycatcher, white fronted nunbird or even the long tailed tyrant (the only member of genus *Colonia*).

Just south of Limón look for the **Río Vizcaya bridge**. There is a turn just before the bridge leading to the river mouth which is an easy spot for observing shorebirds.

Cahuita National Park is another birders' dream. Swamps, forest and beaches hold green ibis, yellow-crowned night herons, northern boat-billed herons, Swainson toucans, keel-billed toucans, rufous kingfishers, and the Central American curassow, among other curious birds.

From Manzanillo there is **a trail that leads south through old cacao plantations** skirting the beach in dramatic fashion towards Punta Mona. This is a fantastic walk where you can expect to see a thicket antpitta, plain-colored tanager, emerald tanager and perhaps even a sulphur-rumped tanager. Cool!

SURFING
Costa Rica is justifiably one of the top surfing destinations in the world. There are four or five primary hot spots you'll see surfers heading for with boards strapped to the tops of their SUVs.

There are a few spots near Limón, Westphalia, Playa Bonita, and Portete, but things are much cooler further south. **Black Beach** near Cahuita is popular, as is Manzanillo. But the king of them all is a tough walk south of Manzanillo: the famous **Salsa Brava**, one wicked wave in the Caribbean south of Cahuita, in an area of dreadlocks, spliffs and curried goat. Don't miss it.

7. NORTH-CENTRAL COSTA RICA

Northwest of San José lies a region of spectacular mountains, several of which are **active volcanoes**. Here the continental divide slopes down to the Pacific Ocean. You'll pass through many different ecosystems, from lush cloud forests to drier coastal forest. The **Monteverde Cloud Forest Reserve** and the **Arenal volcano** are Costa Rica's most popular tourist destinations. Little visited **Rincón de la Vieja** features an enormous crater and dozens of bubbling pools.

From the airport, you may be able to reach Arenal or Monteverde before dark if you can manage to get out of San José before noon. Rincón is going to take overnight unless you fly into Liberia. If you arrive in the country on an afternoon flight you can arrange for a car and driver ahead of time to take you directly from the airport to your lodge. I don't recommend doing a nighttime drive by rental car.

Due to distance and bad roads, it's not really practical to visit Arenal or Monteverde on a one-day trip from either San José or Nicoya, but if you are staying in one of the lodges near Monteverde or Fortuna (the town closest to Arenal), there are dozens of ways to spend a day. Seemingly hundreds of activities, represented by a similar number of glossy brochures, attract visitors.

COORDINATES
Arenal and Monteverde are about 4 hours northwest of San José and Rincón de la Vieja is another two or three hours. All three areas are actually more easily accessible from Liberia and the Nicoya Peninsula.

ONE GREAT DAY AROUND ARENAL
If you have one day to spend in the area of **Arenal volcano** (see photo on previous page), rise early to take advantage of any clearing in the cloud cover that might occur first thing in the morning. With luck you'll be able to enjoy breakfast at your lodge, with a view of the cone just past your cornflakes or *gallo pinto* (rice and beans, a typical Tico breakfast).

On a nice day, the volcano is observable from hundreds of vantage points, including from the streets of Fortuna. The nicer places to stay are lodges well outside Fortuna, closer to the cone. **Fortuna** is a smallish, bustling town with one purpose: booking and managing tourist activities in the area. It's not a particularly great place to hang out.

Perhaps the best views, especially at night, are from the bridge past **Tabacón** near the entrance to **Arenal Observatory Lodge**. There is a small gravel parking area. You'll know the place because there will be a number of other tourists parked there—even a few tour buses. If it is clear, the views from here are great. Be aware that this area is directly in the projected path of any pyroclastic flow the volcano decides to let loose. Toast for slow tourists.

Morning

After breakfast, catch a ride at your hotel for a guided walk through the forest around the volcano, preferably with a trained volcanologist. It will probably rain. Some lodges supply rubber boots and even ponchos. I suggest you bring your own plain, cheap rubber boots. You can buy them at a local hardware store for about $10. You'll certainly hear the mountain rumbling, and you might catch a glimpse through the trees of boulders tumbling down the slopes.

HIGHLIGHTS

• **Arenal Volcano** – The cone is one of the world's most photogenic and active volcanoes.

• **Tabacón Hot Springs** – Soak in the water amid lush greenery.

• **Santa Elena Reserve** – This wonderful wildlife reserve is far less crowded than more famous Monteverde.

• **Rincón de la Vieja Crater** – hot, bubbling mud baths

Afternoon

All the tourists love pricey **Tabacón Hot Springs**, so after lunch explore the spectacular pools and waterfalls amid lush green vegetation, as toucans and macaws fly overhead. There's also a major spa here, offering a variety of treatments, hot stone therapies, massages and yoga lessons.

You could also go on a **hike with a bird specialist guide**. Expect to see three-wattled bellbirds, fasciated tiger herons, sunbitterns, laughing falcons, red-lored parrots, great curassows, northern jacanas, steely-vented hummingbirds, and of course keel-billed toucans. You could still go for a soak in the hot springs before dinner.

Evening

After an afternoon soaking, hiking, or both, I suggest a quiet dinner at your lodge while enjoying a view of the volcano. Unfortunately, I can think of no culinary hotspots in the area. Arenal can put on quite a fiery show at night if the sky is clear. Sometimes, even when things are overcast, you can see an ominous glow in the sky.

ONE GREAT DAY AROUND MONTEVERDE

With only one day in the **Monteverde** and **Santa Elena** area, you'll have to hustle a little to get it all done.

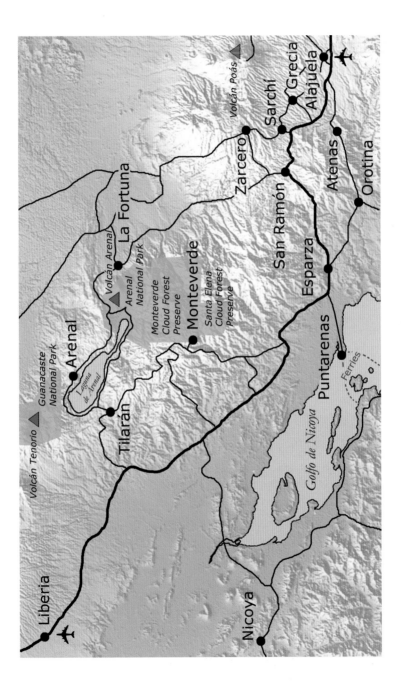

Morning
Skip breakfast at tourist-packed Stella's Bakery and have great snacks at **Moon Shiva** on the main road a little bit closer to Santa Elena. Get a couple of cookies to take with you for later.

Now take the bold step of skipping the world-famous Monteverde Cloud Forest Preserve (known as the "crowd forest" to locals) and go past Santa Elena to the nicer and far less touristed **Santa Elena Cloud Forest Reserve**, where your guide will point out the elusive resplendent quetzal, three-wattled bell bird, and the occasional tinamou.

Downtown Santa Elena offers a couple of decent places to eat. I suggest the **Treehouse** for a burger or pizza with an icy beer or two. But take it easy on the desserts, because after lunch you're going zipping!

Afternoon
After a light meal, it's adrenaline time. All the tourists love zip lines and so-called canopy tours. **Sky Trek** (see photo below) is conveniently located near Santa Elena Cloud Forest Reserve. It is a huge operation with aerial trams, zip lines (wheeeeee!) and elevated walkways through the forest. A lot of people are in and out of this place, and many of them spend part of their time screaming, so you can't expect to see very many animals in the canopy posing for pictures. This is about fun, not nature. You can prob-

ably do something similar in Gatlinburg or Orlando but Costa Rica is famous for zip lines (oops, I mean canopy tours) so go for it.

After excitement and stimulation, educational pursuits can fill the remaining part of the day. Numerous attractions line the strip between Santa Elena and Monteverde, and some of them are worth an hour or so of your time. It is easy to stop in at a serpentarium (snakes), ranarium (frogs), bat jungle, orchid garden, or art gallery.

Just outside the entrance to Monteverde Cloud Forest Preserve is the **Hummingbird Gallery**, a small souvenir shop with dozens of hummingbird feeders in their garden and therefore hundreds of hummingbirds flitting about. It's worth a visit just to watch the aerial daredevils go through their acrobatics. This is a must do for photographers. A very challenging subject, hummingbirds casually pose for tourists here and you are bound to get a few good shots. Turn on your motor drive and "spray and pray."

Just east of Santa Elena is a small botanical garden called **Orquídeas de Monteverde** (Monteverde Orchid Garden). This is a must-see for flower fanatics. Costa Rica is one of the top suppliers of orchids in the world, and the cloud forest habitat is where the most exotic varieties are found. Some of them are quite small, but all are beautiful.

Evening

The **Garden restaurant at Monteverde Lodge** has the best meal in town. Their wine list is good, and their food is better than most of the tourist-filled places in the area. It's expensive, so if you have a bunch of kids or teenagers with you, go to one of the pizza joints instead. They probably wouldn't like the *ceviche* anyway. Nightlife is unremarkable in Monteverde, and you are probably tired after hiking all day anyway, so go back to your lodge and go to bed.

On the other hand, a **nighttime hike** can be a fascinating experience. After dark the creepy-crawly things come out and expose themselves for tourists to view. Most of the lodges can arrange for you to get into the cloud forest at night. If you can find an entomologist (bug person) guide, so much the better.

A FANTASTIC WEEKEND IN NORTH-CENTRAL COSTA RICA

Except for the most frantic tourists, the Arenal area and Monteverde are too far apart to combine a visit to both in the same weekend. The drive between the two areas is roundabout to say the least, and can easily take four or more hours. It's a beautiful drive though. Rincón is actually quite convenient to the airport in Liberia and can be visited from some of the hotels in the Northern Nicoya area.

Arenal offers an awesome volcano, rain forests and hot springs. Stay at one of the lodges around Santa Elena or Arenal, and make day trips to the volcano and one or more of the rain forest preserves in the area.

Monteverde offers cloud forests, canopy tours, zip lines and resplendent quetzals. If you're more interested in experiencing the cloud forest than in hanging around with crowds of other tourists, skip the Monteverde Reserve and visit the Santa Elena Reserve instead.

Rincón de la Vieja offers a huge, semi-active volcanic mountain with at least nine bubbling craters. The national park of the same name is little visited, due to its isolation in the far north of the country, but is well worth a visit. If your interest is in seeing unspoiled rain and cloud forests, avoid Monteverde and visit Rincón instead. Over 350 bird species have been identified.

ARENAL AREA
Friday
You may be able to reach your hotel before dark if you leave the airport before noon. Be sure to plan on volcano watching no matter how late you arrive. With only a weekend and lots of cloudy nights, you need to devote your evenings to hoping for a clear view of the fireworks. I have been to the area three times and I have never seen the volcano in the clear. But I keep going back anyway.

Arenal Observatory Lodge probably has the best nighttime views of the volcano blowing off. Even if it's too cloudy to actually see anything, the lodge is so close to the volcano it sounds like 747s are taking off all around you. There is a nice, small bar in the lodge where you can sit and watch the lava.

Saturday
Hike rain forests on the volcano slopes in the morning. Plan on rain, mud and howler monkeys. A wide variety of tours and hikes are available. I suggest working with your hotel to select a morning guide.

Best Views of the Lava Show

For years the best view of the fiery action was from the west, which made Arenal Observatory Lodge one of the best viewing points. But lava flow changes and, for awhile, AOL lost its vantage point. A new change in flow makes the lodge once again the best hotel in the area for nighttime lava viewing.

Plan on spending the afternoon at **Tabacón** or nearby **Baldi Hot Springs**. The springs and the nearby Tabacón Lodge are rumored to have been built directly on top of the lava flow from the last major eruption, now covered with jungle foliage. When the volcano blows again, the pyroclastic flow is scheduled to come right through the valley where these two lovely tourist destinations have been built. In other words: you could be toast.

The springs and surrounding plantings are very, very nice. This is not simply another cheesy roadside tourist attraction. However, their already high prices continue to climb steadily and, as so often happens with popularity, quality suffers. I have recently been hearing complaints about poor food and inconsiderate service. On my visits, I found it to be overcrowded and overpriced but still enjoyable.

Tabacón is not the only hot spring in the area. Baldi Hot Springs may not be quite as beautiful as Tabacón, lacking the picturesque waterfalls, but it does have 10 pools at different temperatures, a fully-equipped spa, a restaurant and a couple of swim-up bars. The vegetation is similarly lush, and there's a view of the Arenal cone.

The prices are similar and the crowds much smaller. Another bonus is that Baldi is located outside of the official Risk Zones, so you can swim in peace, without the fear of being incinerated.

Sunday

Arenal.net runs a variety of tours in the Arenal region, including trips to the volcano, rafting and zip line canopy tours. Their web site has lots of information about the volcano, including some astounding photos of eruptions.

For a truly special perspective, take their horseback trip over the wonderful **Caño Negro Trail** from Arenal to Monteverde. You'll climb through the cloud forest, over the 4,500-foot Continental Divide, with amazing views of the volcano and the lake ($75 per person, including pickup from your hotel and a light lunch).

MONTEVERDE AREA
Friday
The drive to Monteverde is one of tourism's most famous **bone jarring rides**. High in the mountains, there are only three winding, looping routes into Monteverde and all are only partially paved. Although the actual amount of driving that has to be done on the unpaved portion is only about 20 miles, it is an especially bumpy, bouncy, rattling trip. The problem is not so much the mud as it is the rocks. The road surface is composed of millions of baseball- and softball-size rocks. It is impossible to go more than a couple of miles an hour, and you still come out of the trip with your head buzzing. Large buses, trucks, motorcycles and other local traffic ignore this dilemma and seem to pass at speeds more appropriate for Interstate highways. In the dry season, clouds of dust can be oppressive. It's about a three or four hour trip from San José, and three hours or so from Arenal around the lake.

If you are lucky enough to stay at the **Monteverde Lodge**, you will be able to enjoy their bar and large Jacuzzi for an evening soak before bed. Before retiring, I would also arrange for a guide for the next day to Santa Elena Cloud Forest Reserve to look for a resplendent quetzal or two.

Saturday
Leave the hotel bright and early (or even earlier) for a guided trip to **Santa Elena Cloud Forest Reserve**. I prefer it to the more popular Monteverde Cloud Forest Preserve because it is much less crowded and offers pretty much the same environment and sights. If I had the time, I would enthusiastically visit both!

After lunch at one of the cool eateries that have sprung up all over town, you probably won't be able to resist the lure of the zip lines and canopy tours. If you must do the zip line thing, try not to scream. Zip lines are available in almost all parts of the country. Realize that although some operators call their thing a "canopy tour," you don't get much time to actually examine the canopy, and most wildlife will be miles away from where tourists go screaming through the jungle. And we do scream.

Sunday

It may take you the bulk of the day to get back to San José or the Liberia area. But if you have time, don't waste the morning. Go to whichever park you visited yesterday with a guide or whichever park you did not have time to get to by yourself—no guide this time. Get there early, walk slowly, and listen to the howler monkeys. You can also visit some of the educational attractions on the strip between Monteverde and Santa Elena such as the **Ranaria** (frog house), **Bat Jungle** or **Butterfly Garden**.

RINCÓN AREA

Friday

This area is quite close to the airport in Liberia and, if you are staying in one of the Nicoya resorts, can be visited for an overnight or weekend side trip. All of the three lodges mentioned here offer transportation from the Liberia airport and can arrange for transport from Monteverde and Arenal. You are likely to check into your lodge just about dark, so I suggest a drink at the bar after dinner to meet your fellow guests and lodge staff.

Saturday

There are three great parks in this part of the country but with only a weekend you will have to pick one.

Rincón de la Vieja National Park has nine volcanoes, with the large and active **Rincón de la Vieja** (the crater is some 15 km wide), and several inactive ones, including **Santa Maria**. A short hike from park headquarters is the **Blue Lagoon**, an exquisite swimming lake with a waterfall and a hot spring.

Caño Negro National Wildlife Refuge is a vast region of wetlands beloved of serious birders around the world. This is one of the more likely places in the country to spot a jaguar.

Guanacaste National Park was created to serve as a wildlife corridor between nearby Santa Rosa National Park and the Orosí and Cacao volcanoes. There are precipitous trails to the summit of the **Cacao Volcano**.

Any of these three parks will take most of the day for a cursory exploration. Your lodge may be able to arrange for a night hike. I strongly suggest trying to arrange this, as you will see an entirely different set of creatures than the ones you have been looking at all day.

Sunday

You may be able to squeeze in a visit to one of the parks before heading back to Liberia or your lodge in Nicoya. The ride back can be done in a couple of hours, so it is certainly practical to try to have some more fun on your last day in the area.

ONE WEEK IN NORTH-CENTRAL COSTA RICA

With a week to spend in this region, you can easily visit **Arenal** and **Monteverde** (or the less crowded cloud forest preserve of **Santa Elena**). You could also get in some windsurfing or kiteboarding on **Lake Arenal**, and spend some time hanging around the fun town of Santa Elena.

There are several large and remote parks in the northwest part of the country, far from the tourist hordes. Take your time in Monteverde and Arenal, follow the weekend plan for both of these great destinations, then go a little way off the beaten path to the other parks below—you'll be rewarded with spectacular volcano action and wonderful wildlife. You may have time to check out rarely-visited **Rincón de la Vieja** with its bubbling craters.

Arenal

Arenal is one of the world's most active volcanoes, and its conical shape is just what you'd expect. It spouts forth lava, smoke and noxious gases on a regular basis, and can be heard for miles around, sounding like a jet plane.

At night it's just like the fireworks in Sydney harbor. Bright red lava spews down the sides of the cone while glowing, freight-car-size globs of burning, noxious lava are disgorged into the air like Roman candles. Getting to see the fun during the day is a rare treat, as the summit is almost always covered by clouds. Early in the morning is your best bet.

Arenal Observatory Lodge has a very nice view of the volcano from their dining room. The lodge is close to the volcano, with trails leading as close to the cone itself as you are allowed to go (not too close). Keep in mind that as Arenal is in the rain forest, it is usually obscured by clouds (that's where the rain comes from), so many visitors never actually get to see the cone. But the surrounding rain forest is worth the trip all by itself.

Arenal is a *stratovolcano*, which means one that has built up in layers over the years, each eruption adding a new layer of ashes and lava. It's part of the so-called "Ring of Fire," a chain of volcanoes that surrounds the coasts of the Pacific Ocean, where adjoining tectonic plates have crashed together, releasing molten magma from deep beneath the Earth's surface.

The last major eruption (meaning one that forced the local people to evacuate) happened in 2000. Another big one occurred in 1968. Minor eruptions and spewage happen all the time, with an occasional bit of pyroclastic flow—this means an avalanche of rocks and boulders that can move at up to 50 miles per hour and (according to the US Geological Survey) "will destroy nearly everything in its path." You don't want to be in the area if this starts happening. See *volcanoes.usgs.gov* for lots more information on volcanoes.

Arenal Volcano National Park features a number of trails from which you can see various types of volcanic action, as well as fields of lava and other evidence of past eruptions. The volcano itself isn't the only attraction: the cloud forest that covers the slopes has the usual variety of wildlife, and you can swim in a crystal-clear waterfall, surrounded by tropical greenery. *Info: Open 8am-4pm. Entry: $10 adults; $1 under 12. Tel. 2461-8499.*

If you'd like to get a little off the typical tourist path, and learn a lot about Costa Rican wildlife, pay a visit to **Proyecto Asis**, near Fortuna. Their wildlife rescue center rehabilitates all kinds of critters that have been rescued from the animal trade. Some are permanent residents, and others are released back to the wild. They also run a Spanish school, and offer long-term volunteering opportunities. Desafío Adventure Company runs guided tours to Proyecto Asís, as well as rafting and other adventure tours. You can also visit on your own, but they ask that you contact them ahead of time. *Info: www.institutoasis.com; Tel. 2475-9121, 2475-6696.*

Monteverde

Straddling the continental divide, the **Monteverde Cloud Forest Preserve** is one of the most popular tourist destinations in the country. Fortunately, it is big. Otherwise the crush of tourists would have destroyed the charm of the park long ago. The park is so popular that, almost every day, all day, park officials are forced to limit the number of visitors, causing tourists to line up waiting for someone to exit the park before they are allowed to enter. Monteverde always seems to be overflowing with fanny pack-wearing gringos and their sticky kids wearing mouse ears.

There is a good reason for all this popularity: the park has wonderful vistas, extensive wildlife, unusual bird life and easy-to-walk, well-marked trails. It is known as one of the best places to see the elusive resplendent quetzal—a spectacular, long-tailed bird. The last time I was there, I hired a private guide to take me, alone, through the park on a morning tour. We were never completely alone on the crowded trails and, when my guide

spotted a quetzal, we were quickly joined by at least 40 others jostling to get a look at the bird. I quickly moved on down the trail.

There are 13 km of paths open to day hikers. **Guided walks** with local nature guides are available. You can take a morning or a night walk for about $15 per person. **Advance reservations are wise.** When it gets crowded, they close the paths, and you'll have to wait until someone else comes out before you can go in. Reserving a guided tour will eliminate that possibility. There's a visitors' center with a small restaurant and gift shop.

Costa Rica Expeditions, which owns Monteverde Lodge, has a good reputation for providing particularly well-trained guides. If you have limited time, I suggest visiting **Santa Elena Cloud Forest Reserve** instead of the better-known Monteverde Cloud Forest Preserve (known as the "crowd forest" to locals). The sights are just about the same and there are far fewer tourists. If you can, definitely visit both.

Don't miss a visit to the **Hummingbird Garden**, a small tourist shop right outside the gate to the Monteverde Cloud Forest Preserve. They have a dozen or so hummingbird feeders set up and the little critters buzz around in the hundreds—quite a sight!

If you don't like crowds, head to less overrun parks like Santa Elena Cloud Forest Reserve or **Rincón de la Vieja** (see below) to enjoy the rain forests and wildlife in relative peace and quiet. The restaurants and lodges in this area can seem impersonal compared to other parts of the country that see fewer visitors.

The **cheese factory** is one of those "attractions" that everybody talks about, and it has some slight historical relevance (cheese making is the traditional industry of the Quakers who founded the town of Monteverde in the 1950s), but there is nothing of interest here except some (good) cheese for sale. You can't actually tour the factory or anything.

To enjoy the cloud forests and flavor of the area without the crowds and tourist trappings, visit **Ecolodge San Luis**. This tropical biology research station, run by the University of Georgia, welcomes visitors, and has a few cabinas and bungalows available for overnight stays. If you're seriously interested in tropical ecology, this is a must. It is located a little downhill from Monteverde in its own cloudy valley, yet convenient to town in case you feel the need for more prosaic tourist activities. I love the place and always seem to leave with good friends I didn't have before. Info: www. crica.com/hotels/sanluis.

Santa Elena Cloud Forest Reserve

Far smaller than adjacent Monteverde Cloud Forest Preserve (310 hectares versus 10,000), this park sees far fewer visitors. This makes it much the better choice for a visit. The sights and the facilities are similar, and the tourist hordes don't seem to have discovered it yet.

The last time I was at Santa Elena Cloud Forest Reserve, a half-tame peccary was wandering around the entrance to the park posing for pictures. I hadn't taken 10 steps down the trail when my guide softly said, "there's a quetzal" and pointed to a nearby tree. The three-wattled bellbird was not much further along. On a three-hour hike, I encountered only two other groups of hikers. The day before in Monteverde I was never out of sight or hearing of other groups of bird venerators.

There are four trails, with a total length of 12 km. The **South Youth Challenge Trail** leads to an observation tower and a couple of scenic overlooks. Santa Elena also has views of the Arenal volcano. The spectacular **Caño Negro Trail** climbs over the mountains, passing through several different ecosystems along the way and affording views of the volcano and the lake.

As at Monteverde, the visitors' center has a small café and a gift shop, and guided walks are available (two daily and one at night, about $15 per person). You can easily enjoy the park in just a couple of hours or spend an entire morning or afternoon.

Santa Elena

This crowded but pleasant little tourist town has lots of bars, restaurants, tourist shops, art galleries, discos and lodging places along the strip that runs between the town and the park. The road is a spectacularly rutted mud and gravel affair that goes about three miles from the park to town. Traffic jams outside Santa Elena can mean a quarter-mile line of SUVs and tourist buses creeping into town. Many park well outside town and walk in. Tourists zoom around annoyingly on rental four wheelers and popular lunch spots are often jammed.

The strip is rapidly becoming clogged shoulder-to-shoulder with tourist "attractions" and will probably soon resemble some of the more notorious tourist areas in the US.

However, some of the animal-oriented attractions are quite worthwhile. At the **Ranario**, near Monteverde Lodge, you can see some of the colorful local frogs (tip: it's more interesting at night).

The **Bat Jungle has**—you guessed it—bats! Here you can see and hear several species of the fascinating mammals (Costa Rica has over 100 species) zooming around and going about their normal activities. Richard Laval, who created the exhibits, often leads tours.

Another favorite is the **Butterfly Garden** (*Jardín de Mariposas*), near the Pension Monteverde Inn. Everyone loves the resplendent butterflies, and you'll also see a variety of other insects, from giant tarantulas to tiny but industrious leafcutter ants.

Sabine's Smiling Horses offers a variety of horseback tours in the Monteverde area. Ride through coffee plantations to beautiful waterfalls and viewpoints over Nicoya Bay.

Rincón de la Vieja National Park

Here, in a little-visited part of the country, are all sorts of otherworldly volcanic landscapes, including a lake that's steaming hot and others that are ice cold. There are puddles of boiling mud, and vents that spew sulfur dioxide and acid clouds (what fun!). There are sulfurous hot springs you can bathe in, and others that you definitely don't want to bathe in, or even walk too close to.

This park incorporates **nine volcanoes**, including the large and active **Rincón de la Vieja** (the crater is some 15 km wide), and several inactive ones, including **Santa Maria**, at 1,916 meters one of the highest peaks in the region. It's surprising that the park is not better-known and crowded, especially as it's only a short drive from Liberia.

What is a Cloud Forest?

As moisture-filled warm air blows in from the Pacific Ocean, it meets the high mountains of the continental divide, and condenses to form clouds. Visitors see a forest mysteriously **shrouded in fog**. The 100% humidity and over four meters of rain every year create an incredibly lush flora. Damp-loving **lichens** and **mosses** cover every inch of available space. Trees are draped with epiphytes (plants that grow in trees, such as **bromeliads** and **orchids**), creating an entire ecosystem high in the forest canopy. Many animals spend their entire lives up here, and you won't see them from the ground. Some parks feature platforms high up in the canopy, where visitors can try to get a glimpse of some of these tree-dwellers. Don't worry about clambering up a ladder—visitors are usually raised and lowered by means of ropes and pulleys. It's well worth a visit to one of these **canopy platforms**. The patient visitor may be rewarded by a sight of arboreal monkeys or sloths, but most of the time you'll simply see a lot of **LBBs**—little brown birds—and perhaps some interesting insects.

One of the most popular spots is the **Blue Lagoon**, a 30-minute hike from park headquarters. This exquisite swimming lake has a waterfall and a hot spring. Minerals in the rocks make the lake bright blue.

There are well-marked trails throughout the park. However, for safety's sake, and to learn about the unique ecology of the region, it's best to visit with a guide, which you can organize through any of the lodges in the region.

All sorts of wildlife are abundant. You may see a peccary, wild goat, tayra (a sleek weasel-like carnivore) or collared anteater, as well as three species of monkeys. If you're lucky, you might even see a pussycat. You'll certainly see some of the over 350 species of birds and beautiful **morpho butterflies**. The trees and vines are dense with epiphytes, including the national flower, the **purple orchid**.

This park is also a capital place for horseback riding and mountain biking. You can easily rent bikes, or arrange for horseback trips, in Liberia.

The tourist crowds haven't discovered Rincón de la Vieja. The area's lodges are comfortable and not yet crowded. I suggest cutting short your stay in Monteverde and spending at least two nights exploring the forests around the cones. *Info: There are two ranger stations: Santa María, Northeast of Liberia; and Las Pailas, near Curubandé. Both are open 8am-4pm daily, and can arrange guided tours. Camping is available. Admission is $10. Tel. 2661-8139.*

Caño Negro National Wildlife Refuge

Caño Negro is a vast (25,100 acres) area of wetlands, which becomes a lake during the rainy season. It's a paradise for **waterfowl**, as well as one of the more likely places in the country to spot a **jaguar**. Twitchers should expect sightings of glossy ibis, black-necked stilt, neotropical cormorants, American anhinga, northern jacana, American widgeon, wood stork, white ibis, black-bellied tree duck, cattle egret, northern shoveler, snail kite, green backed heron, Nicaraguan grackle, roseate spoonbill, and blue-winged teal (and you're sure to see crocodiles and caimans, which keep the birdies in check). The forests and grasslands are home to cougars, jaguars, ocelots, tapirs, peccaries and three species of monkeys.

There are no tourist facilities—this is a refuge rather than a park. Everything needs to be done by boat. There are no trails. Fishing for snook, gar and giant tarpon is reputed to be excellent. Fishing season is from July 1 to March 31. There are no guides but, if you have your own tackle, small canoes can be hired. There are plentiful bull sharks so no swimming! *Info: There is no cost to enter the reserve. A fishing license is $30 from the ranger station in Caño Negro village. The reserve is open to visitors around the clock. The ranger station is open 8am-4pm Monday to Friday. Tel. 2471-1309.*

Guanacaste National Park

This 80,000 acre park was created in 1989 as a corridor between Santa Rosa National Park and the Orosí and Cacao volcanoes, allowing birds and mammals to migrate between coastal and cloud forest habitats. Wide-ranging species such as jaguars and mountain lions make local seasonal migrations between the dry forest and the evergreen cloud and rain forests. You can emulate the pumas, ocelots, peccaries, capuchin monkeys, howlers and coatis, and hike a trail that passes through several elevations and many different ecosystems. From some of the high lookout points, you can see the Lake of Nicaragua to the north and the Pacific Ocean to the west.

The Cacao Sector has precipitous trails to the summit of the **Cacao Volcano**. The Maritza Sector includes the continental divide, and the headwaters of several rivers, as well as dozens of ancient petroglyphs strewn through the jungle. The most remote area of the park is the Pitilla Sector, which has hiking trails to the Orosí Volcano. There are **three biological research stations** in the park: Cacao, Maritza and Pitilla. All are near **Potrerillos**, which is about 20 miles north of Liberia on the Interamerican highway. All are open to visitors, and have basic dormitory-style lodging available for tour groups. *Info: Admission is $10.*

BEST SLEEPS & EATS
BEST SLEEPS IN FORTUNA/ARENAL
Tabacón Lodge $$$

This lodge is conveniently just up the street from the famous hot springs, but is said to be directly in the path of any serious Arenal eruption. The lodge is built on top of the lava flow from the last big one. **Pyroclastic flows** from new eruptions are scheduled to blast right through the valley, incinerating everything. Baked tourists, anyone? The rooms are comfortable, but the restaurant has been getting poor reviews lately. The as-

sociated hot springs across the street are expensive, but room prices sometimes include access to the springs. *Info: www.tabacon.com; Tel. 2519-1999, 877/277-8291 US.*

Boring Fortuna

Fortuna is an uninteresting tourism-support town, which is **useful for booking tours** if you don't have everything arranged before you get to the area. It's a little far from the volcano, and has no particular charms of its own. Most people prefer to stay somewhere closer to the volcano, where they might see some action if the clouds ever clear up. The interesting places to stay are on the way to the lake, towards the town of Nuevo Arenal and beyond. Most lodges can help you arrange any of the local tours and activities. Without a car, transportation can be a bit of a problem.

Arenal Observatory Lodge $

Originally built as a research station for volcanologists, Arenal Observatory Lodge is a good lower-priced choice. Rooms are comfortable but basic, and some have **spectacular views of the cone**. They have a great pool and handicapped-accessible jungle trails. The restaurant and bar are good, with a nice view, but are not really very exciting for the price.

The lodge is set in a heavily forested area with lots of howler monkeys. A very good **guided jungle walk** near the cone is included in the room price. The **howler monkeys** wake you up in the morning if the volcano doesn't. This is a good base for exploring around the volcano, and is the closest hotel to the cone. The site is across a small valley from the main flow of lava and is therefore considered to be out of harm's way in the event of a major eruption. You're close to the action but presumably safe from random pyroclastic flows. This lodge is **my favorite place to stay in the area**. I have heard reports lately that the direction of lava flow from the cone has changed, and that the nightly light shows put on by the volcano have shifted to the other side of the cone. You should check with the hotel before booking, or you may miss the performance. *Info: www. arenalobservatorylodge.com; Tel. 2290-7011, 2479-1070.*

BEST SLEEPS IN MONTEVERDE/SANTA ELENA

The variety of lodging in the Monteverde/Santa Elena area is huge, and the comfort level runs from bunkhouses to quite comfortable. The quality level ends just before luxury. There are **no true luxury lodges** or multi-star hotels.

Monteverde Lodge $$$

Thousands of **bromeliads** infest the delightfully landscaped grounds around the most comfortable place to stay in Monteverde. This lodge is a little away from the dusty strip, and is quiet, with a wonderful view all the way down over the cloud forest slopes to the Pacific and Nicoya Peninsula. The rooms are contemporary and well maintained. There's no AC, but you won't miss it, as nights up here are generally cool.

This is one of several lodges run by **Costa Rica Expeditions**, which does a first-class job of arranging for certified guides to all the local places of interest. When I stay here, I simply put myself in their hands and let them make all my tour arrangements.

I found the tour prices to be the same as I would be likely to pay when not going through the lodge. I recently booked a tour through the lodge to Santa Elena at the price of $15 per person. In the morning when I met the guide I found that I was the only person going. When the wonderful tour was over the guide informed me that the price was $15. I know this is the going rate, but I doubled it since it lasted three hours and a little. I had assumed I would be paying for a personal guide if I were the only participant. The guide did a wonderful job helping me to see quetzals and three-wattled bellbirds.

The restaurant is expensive but very good. Seafood, steaks and chicken are creatively prepared. Be sure to try their *ceviche*. There is a good selection of Chilean and Spanish wines, with all price categories covered well. *Info: www.monteverdelodge.com; Tel. 2257-0766, 2521-6099.*

Hotel Belmar $$$

Perched on a forested hillside with views stretching all the way to the Nicoya Peninsula and the Pacific Ocean, the Belmar is a consistent favorite. The rooms are charming, all in rich hardwood, with large, comfortable beds and  nice balconies. The chalet, next to the hotel, features luxurious rooms with huge windows right in the jungle canopy—some have private Jacuzzis.

There's also a **large Jacuzzi** for all guests, where you can soak after a day's hiking and look out into the green. Massages, spa treatments and yoga classes are on offer, and organic fruity delights are whipped up in the juice bar. The restaurant serves a hearty breakfast (included) and a healthy and interesting range of international resort cuisine.

The Belmar is surrounded by **lush grounds**, and you can take a nice little hike right on the property to prepare for wildlife-watching in nearby Monteverde. This is a true eco-lodge; solar water heating, recycling and serving local organic produce earned the Belmar the **Certificate for Sustainable Tourism** from the Costa Rica Tourism Board. *Info: www.belmarmonteverde.com; Tel. 2645-5201, 866/978-6424 US.*

Ecolodge San Luis and Research Station $$

If you are interested in tropical ecology and would like to hang out with researchers and students, Ecolodge San Luis is the most interesting place to stay and explore the surrounding forest as well as the parks and sights around Monteverde. Twitchers and power birders love it, adding significantly to their life lists. Tourists with $700 titanium walking sticks and space-age water bottles rub shoulders with college professors and backpackers.

The lodge is a little off the beaten path, but still very close to the park. In fact, it is a full-time tropical biology research station, operated by the University of Georgia, and almost always has students and instructors on site involved in various university-level **tropical biology research** projects. Guests are encouraged to participate. The atmosphere provided by having the students there, with classes and projects going on, makes for a refreshing break from the nearby tourist mania in Monteverde. The guides are usually students who take visitors to see their projects, on horseback rides, and on hikes through the cloud forest.

The food is great, but the rooms are spartan. There is a choice between dormitory bunks, small cabins or individual rooms. Prices vary, of course. The higher-priced rooms are comfortable if plain. There is hot water. If you are interested in serious ecological studies or just want to get the real lowdown on the area, this is the only place to stay. I like to stay outside Monteverde in the Ecolodge San Luis and drive to town only when I have to. Prices include all meals and most activities. *Info: www.uga.edu/costarica; Tel. 2645-7363.*

BEST SLEEPS AROUND RINCÓN

The Rincón area would be a good destination if you want to escape the tourist hordes of Monteverde/Arenal and enjoy rain forests and volcanoes without a crowd of other hikers on your heels. It's quite close to the international airport at Liberia, which might make a good alternative to flying into San José.

Hacienda-Lodge Guachipelín $$

Down-to-earth yet comfortable, this 50-room hotel is well situated to enjoy the attractions of the nearby park and the northern Guanacaste region of Costa Rica. It is located at the foot of the Rincón de la Vieja volcano, adjacent to the national park. Natural hot springs, rain forests, jungle waterfalls and volcanic mud pots are all close by. You can also enjoy the steam vents with their "unmistakable smell." A **four-hour hike to the crater** is offered every day.

The lodge is within a working cattle ranch, with large areas set aside for protection. This is a good place to stay if you are interested in horseback activities. They offer multi-day rides in the area around the park. There is a pool with natural spring water. *Info: www.guachipelin.com; Tel. 2690-2900.*

> **Nice Places, Some Bugs**
> Most visitors to the Arenal and Monteverde area don't come for luxury. They come to explore and learn about the rain and cloud forests and to see volcanoes, preferably erupting vigorously. **Expect musty jungle smells and bugs** in what are otherwise nice places. In the jungle, the bugs have been winning the war since dinosaur days. Don't be surprised to find ants in even the cleanest and most well run upscale lodgings.

Rinconcito Lodge $
Located close to Rincón de la Vieja as well as Miravalles Volcano, Rinconcito ("little corner") is a small lodge **specializing in organizing activities** for guests including horseback riding, trips to bubbling springs, mud baths, boiling mud pots, hot springs, waterfalls, canopy tours, bird watching and other usual rain forest pursuits. Don't expect luxury at $35 per night for a double, but do expect comfort and adventure. The lodge offers transport to and from Liberia airport. *Info: www.rinconcitolodge.com; Tel. 2666-2764.*

BEST EATS AROUND FORTUNA/ARENAL
This area is much more about nature and the cone than fine dining, so leave your gourmet at home and eat in your lodge, or try one of the great Tico *sodas* for a *casado*.

Rancho Paraíso Steak House $$
This is a proper steak house, nothing fancy but a really great selection of steaks including some from Argentina. Most of the steaks are a little tougher than what you would expect back home since most of the local beef is grass raised. The fancy stuff is exported, but the Rancho Paraíso has some good ones. Skip the house red. *Info: On the way out of town towards the cone, on the right. Tel. 2460-5333.*

La Vaca Muca $
For a solid Costa Rican *casado*, or plate lunch/dinner, this is a winner. Your choice of beef, chicken, fish or other local specialty comes with countless vegetable side dishes. Shady roadside places like this serve pretty much the same thing you get in the tourist lodges for about half the price or less. La Vaca Muca is a particularly nice one. *Info: On the way out of town towards the cone on the left.*

BEST EATS AROUND MONTEVERDE
This is one of the most touristed areas of the country, and that fact is reflected in the dining situation. There are dozens of tourist-oriented restaurants, and most of the hotels have reasonable restaurants. But none of them are at all cheap and most are crowded with—you guessed it—tourists. The **service can sometimes be aloof**, impersonal, or even downright bad.

The Garden $$$

This is the **best restaurant in town**, although it's a little pricey. The creative menu changes daily and often has a couple of things not on most of the tourist lodge tables. The *ceviche* is usually interesting. The wine list is good, with several levels of Chilean and Spanish wines to choose from. Views out over a cloud-swept valley are nice if you can get a table at a window. There is a small, pleasant bar. *Info: In Monteverde Lodge. Tel. 2257-0766.*

Stella's $$

Stella's bakery, on the strip between Santa Elena and Monteverde, bakes **wonderful breads, cakes** etc. On a piece of paper, you check what you want on your sandwich with which kind of bread and everything and they whip it up for you. There is almost always a long line of tourists loading up on sandwiches and sticky buns. The service can be snotty, but the food is good. *Info: About halfway between Santa Elena and the park entrance. Tel. 2645-5560.*

Treehouse Café and Internet $$

Upstairs on the main street in Santa Elena, close to the grocery store, the Treehouse is a shady and relatively quiet place to have a nice lunch. They  feature quite good hamburgers (with ham!) pizzas, chicken and extreme milkshakes. It is aimed directly at tourists but that's okay, because we are tourists and we like a hamburger or pizza from time to time. Get a balcony seat and watch the action on the street below: budget travelers staggering under huge orange backpacks, ball cap-and-t-shirt-clad families in SUVs with four kids still red-faced and screaming fresh from the zip lines, and behatted twitchers with spotting scopes clutching battered copies of *The Birds of Costa Rica*. I love it.

Chunches, also in Santa Elena, is well known as an interesting bookstore/laundromat/children's stuff store. In Costa Rican Spanish, *chunches* means "things" or "stuff."

BEST EATS AROUND RINCON

Outside of the lodges, there is very little restaurant activity in the area.

Hacienda-Lodge Guachipelín $$

The lodge restaurant has basic a la carte selections and a good, *típico* buffet. *Info: www.guachipelin.com; Tel.2690-2900.*

BEST SPORTS & RECREATION AROUND ARENAL

Proyecto Asis

This wildlife rescue center rehabilitates animals and birds that have been rescued from the animal trade. They also run a Spanish school, and offer long-term volunteering opportunities. Desafio Adventure Company runs guided tours to Proyecto Asis, as well as rafting and other adventure tours. You can also visit on your own, but they ask that you contact them ahead of time. *Info: www.institutoasis.com; Tel. 2475-9121.*

Arenal.net

This agency offers a variety of tours in the Arenal region, including trips to the volcano, rafting and zip line canopy tours. Their web site has lots of information about the volcano, including some astounding photos of eruptions. For a truly special perspective, take their horseback trip over the wonderful **Caño Negro Trail** from Arenal to Monteverde. You'll

climb through the cloud forest, over the 4,500-foot Continental Divide, with amazing views of the volcano and the lake ($75 per person, including pickup from your hotel and a light lunch). *Info: www.arenal.net; Tel. 888/456-3212 US.*

Tabacón Hot Springs

Pricey Tabacón seems to be on every tourist's hot list, and the waterfalls and landscaping are quite impressive, so don't let me stop you. I suggest you try to work it out to eat somewhere else. *Info: Open 11am-10pm. Full day $49 adults; $27 kids (4-9). They also offer package deals including lunch or dinner. Some hotels offer discounted tickets for guests. www.tabacon.com; Tel. 2519-1999, 877/277-8291 US.*

Baldi Hot Springs

Baldi is a family-oriented water park that's a little safer and much less expensive than the nearby competition. They have three swim-up bars, two waterslides, restaurant, spa, and changing rooms. Created by visionary entrepreneur Mr. Alberto Rodríguez Baldí, the springs have been expanded over the years into one of the area's top attractions. *Info: Open 10am-10pm. Entrance is $28, or $45 including lunch or dinner. Children five and under half-price. www.arenal.net/Baldi-hot-springs.htm; Tel. 2645-7070.*

FISHING

Freshwater fishing for exotic local species such as *machaca*, *guapote* (a relative of the peacock bass) and *mojara* is action-packed.

Captain Ron's Lake Arenal Fishing Tours
American Ron Saunders offers fishing trips on Arenal in his 18-foot Boston Whaler. He provides all gear for conventional, spin, or fly fishing. His half- or full-day trips include everything. And I mean everything: bait, tackle, beer, food, and cigars. He will do a pick up and drop off at your hotel. What a deal! *Info: www.arenalfishing.com; Tel. 8339-3345.*

WINDSURFING & KITEBOARDING
Lake Arenal is one of the world's top spots for windsurfing, thanks to a constant wind that averages 20 mph during the peak season (November through January). Any time during this period, you'll see radical windsurfers (and even gnarlier youngsters enjoying the latest extreme sport, kiteboarding) getting major air. Most of this action takes place on the west end of the lake past Nuevo Arenal.

Tilawa Windsurf Center
For $500, these guys will provide full lodging and meals along with six days of sailing as much as you want. Sounds exhausting to me. They offer rentals and lessons on a half- or full-day basis. *Info: www.windsurfcostarica. com; Tel. 2692-2002.*

BEST SPORTS & RECREATION AROUND MONTEVERDE AND RINCON
Ranario
Located near Monteverde Lodge, the **Ranario** is a good place to see some of the colorful local frogs you couldn't spot in the cloud forest itself: the marine toad, the colorful poison arrow frog and the famous red eyed tree frog (tip: it's more interesting at night). The tours take about an hour. The guide who showed me through was quite knowledgeable, and was anxious to tell me much more than I ever knew I wanted to know about frogs. *Info: Entry $10. Open 7am–7pm. Tel. 645-6318.*

Bat Jungle
Bruce! It's the Bat Signal! That's right, Robin. The Bat Jungle has—that's right—bats! Here you can see and hear several species of the fascinating mammals (Costa Rica has over 100 species) zooming around and going about their normal activities. Richard Laval, who created the exhibits, often leads tours. 85 live bats are free-flying in the huge enclosure, designed to resemble the cloud forest at night. The enclosure is wired for sound so you can hear the bats echolocating. *Info: On the main road between Santa*

Elena and Monteverde. Open 9am–7:30pm. www.batjungle.com; Tel. 2645-7701.

Butterfly Garden

The Butterfly Garden, also known as Jardín de Mariposas, is near the Monteverde Inn and is a great place to see these elusive little insects up close. Photographers will love it. There are quite a few exhibits in this 15-year-old garden, many of them covering more general cloud forest subjects like leaf cutter ants and a medicinal plant trail. The facility is run completely by volunteers. *Info: www.monteverdebutterflygarden.com; Tel. 2645-5512.*

Orquídeas de Monteverde

This is **a must-see for flower fanatics**. Costa Rica is one of the top suppliers of orchids in the world, and the cloud forest habitat is where the most exotic varieties are found. Some of them are quite small, but all are beautiful. *Info: Open 8am-5pm daily. Entry $5. Tel. 2645-5509.*

HORSEBACK RIDING

Sabine's Smiling Horses

Horseback operations in the Arenal/Monteverde area have a bad reputation for using skinny, broken-down old nags that don't look like they get enough to eat. Sabine offers a variety of horseback tours in the Monteverde area using horses that, if not actually smiling, look like someone who cares takes care of them. Ride through coffee plantations to beautiful waterfalls and viewpoints over Nicoya Bay. You can arrange to travel between Arenal and Monteverde in either direction. Sabine offers tours of the volcano and tours suitable for beginners and children. This is a good one. *Info: www.horseback-riding-tour.com; Tel. 2645-6894.*

ZIP LINES

Selvatura
One of the more popular zip line operators, this is a big place with lots of exhibits including snakes, butterflies and hundreds of screaming tourists on treetop tours. Kids love it. Prices start around $40 per person and go on up from there. *Info: www.selvatour.com; Tel. 2645-5929.*

Original Canopy Tour
There are lots of "original" canopy tours in the world but this was probably the first of the zip companies. They have several locations in Costa Rica and in Puerto Rico. Their "tours" take about two hours including walking to and from the zip line take off point. *Info: Monteverde and Tabacón. www.canopytour.com; Tel. 2291-4465.*

Sky Trek
Conveniently located near Santa Elena Cloud Forest Reserve, Sky Trek is a huge operation with aerial trams, zip lines (wheeeeee!) and elevated walkways through the forest. Very popular with families. *Info: $50-75. www.skytrek.com; Tel. 2479-4100.*

BIRDING

Twitchers have a large choice of destinations where they will be certain to add significantly to their life lists. The most talked-about destination is **Monteverde** to see the **resplendent quetzal**, but it's overrated. There are far too many tourists, and the park is jammed. For that particular bird, a better choice would be the cloud forests around **Chirripó National Park** where you can choose from over 400 bird species including humming-birds, eagle, red-tailed hawk, volcano hummingbird, black guan, crowned wren-thrush, acorn woodpecker, and not just any old trogon but an elegant trogon.

8. THE NORTH PACIFIC COAST

With a somewhat drier climate than other parts of the country, the northern Pacific coast is a favorite destination year-round. The **Nicoya Peninsula has dozens of tiny isolated beach towns**, each with a spectacular strand, and each with its own unique character. This is the place to find your perfect personal beach. Dozens of new resorts have opened up in the last few years offering everything from all-inclusive five star resort living to small, quaint B&Bs.

The **newish international airport** near Liberia has become quite active, with over 20 planeloads of North American tourists a day flying in. It may be a good alternative to flying to San José. Many visitors base themselves in the **beach resort areas** within an hour or two drive of the airport, and indulge in day trips to nearby attractions.

The town of **Liberia** has a rich colonial history and some pretty old buildings, but the modern town is fairly unattractive, and has little more to offer than some US fast-food restaurants and a couple of very run-down motels (although there are several good ones an hour or so away).

Most visitors to this region head for the **Nicoya Peninsula**, a remote and sparsely populated area at the northwest corner of the country. The coast is dotted with tiny towns and spectacular beaches with mountains in the background. Nicoya sees a lot of tourists, but there's a lot of space for them to spread out in, so the region still has a **laid-back**, off-the-beaten-path atmosphere. However, it's slowly but steadily being transformed by real estate developments and new upscale resorts.

If you're heading for the north of the peninsula (**Samara** or **Tamarindo**), going via the new Tempisque Bridge to the north is probably the best route. Another good option, if you're staying at one of the all-inclusive resorts, is simply to fly to one of the small airstrips along the coast, bypassing the roads, which can be dodgy in the rainy season.

The luxury beachfront hotel at **Punta Islita** would be an excellent choice for a base in the area. Another option, more moderately priced, is **Villa**

Alegre. You can spend much of your time lounging on the beach, and make day trips to go fishing, diving or to visit one of the wilderness preserves.

Many of the beach resorts offer all-inclusive packages, with lodging, food, and drinks all included in the price. This is a good option around here, as the most idyllic little beach towns have limited dining options outside the lodges. Of course, most lodges will gladly arrange tours for you as well.

There's quite a nice little website with a lot of useful information about the Nicoya region, and plenty of pictures, at *www.nicoyapeninsula.com*.

COORDINATES
The Nicoya Peninsula occupies the northwest part of the country. Liberia, with a decent international airport, is located at the base of the peninsula.

A FANTASTIC WEEKEND ON THE NORTH PACIFIC COAST
Fly into Liberia, and drive or fly to one of the nearby beachfront resorts, where you can indulge in the full range of coastal activities, and make day trips to the interior. Avid **anglers** should head for **Playa Flamingo**, while wildlife enthusiasts should check out **Santa Rosa National Park** and the **Cabo Blanco** and **Curú Wildlife refuges**. If time permits, spend a day driving up and down the coast, exploring some of the isolated little beaches.

Friday
You can base yourself in one of the various **Nicoya beach resorts** and head up to the rain forest for a long day, especially if you haven't explored the areas around Monteverde and Arenal. But a day relaxing on the beach, and a day visiting nearby national parks or reserves, is a fantastic way to spend your weekend!

You'll probably arrive in the late afternoon or evening. Check out the beach and the hotel bar before bed.

Several beaches feature egg laying sea turtles and you may be able to arrange for a night tour. Just north of Nosara, **Ostional** is famous for the **Ridley turtles** from July to November. Mass turtle landings, *arribadas*, here may be the largest in the world, with as many as a million sea turtle eggs laid on the beach every year.

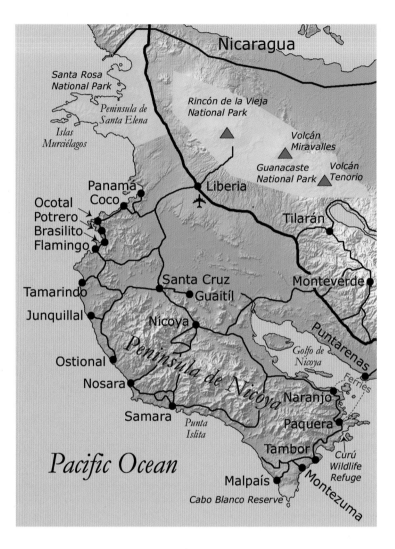

Saturday

Depending on where you are staying, a visit to one of the rain forests or parks is probably going to take most of the day. **Cabo Blanco**, the first park in Costa Rica, is easy to get to from Montezuma or Mal País. If you are staying anywhere near Coco, Flamingo or Tamarindo, you could buzz up to the volcanoes and bubbling mud pools at Rincón de La Vieja.

In most of the resort towns you can arrange for surfing lessons, half-day fishing trips or snorkeling/diving expeditions. The snorkeling is not particularly good in the area due to rough water and low visibility. **Scuba diving can be very rewarding here**. The area is well-known for encounters with manta rays, turtles and sharks. Hard core divers can mingle with man-eating bull sharks.

I have to say that, for me, the best things to do in Nicoya involve walking on the beach, swimming and loafing around in beachside bars. But that's just me.

I recommend trying as hard as you can to find your way to **Camarón Dorado** in Brasilito near the Paradisus Playa Conchal for a great beachside seafood dinner. This is a very romantic spot.

Sunday

Since you only have a weekend, get up early Sunday morning and have a walk on the beach before going back for the breakfast buffet. Depending on your travel plans, you can still fit in a kayaking trip or half-day fishing trip.

If you are driving I suggest a side trip on your way back to the pottery town of **Guaitíl**. This is by far the best place in the country to buy ceramic bowls, tiles, figures, etc. that you see all over in the tourist shops. The potteries are run by women.

ONE WEEK ON THE NORTH PACIFIC COAST

A week in northwestern Costa Rica should give you plenty of time to spend a day **fishing** and a day or two **exploring the rain forests**, without taking too much time away from strenuous activities such as **lying around on the beach** drinking rum. You could divide your time between a couple of different beach resorts, but it probably

makes more sense to pick the one that sounds right for you, and sleep there the whole week. However, be sure to spend a day or two driving along the coast, looking in at the various funky little beaches.

There are many little beach towns, and each has its own character. None of the towns in the Nicoya area is what you could call a major resort, but some are smaller and more laid-back than others. Some beaches are filled with Ticos out for a day's partying at the beach, some are the sites of all-inclusive luxury resorts, some cater to the surfer set, and yet others are the haunts of old hippies going to seed.

Playa del Coco
Playa del Coco (called El Coco on some maps) is a typical little beach town with a main street lined with restaurants and souvenir shops. There's

Great, Deserted Beaches!
The **Nicoya Peninsula has so many miles of great beaches** that, even with beaucoup beachgoers (Tico and tourist) visiting the region, many beaches are all but deserted. A typical Nicoya beach wraps around a crescent bay, framed by towering rocks and backed by lush forest. Many have tiny towns of varying degrees of funkiness, each with its own character. Do you want an upscale resort, or a seedy-but-friendly little spot? A bit of nightlife, or total seclusion? Calm waters for swimming, or a killer break for surfing? Somewhere on the Nicoya Peninsula you can find your perfect beach. The northern region has several luxurious resorts, with championship golf courses and private airstrips. The southern coast is where you'll find the back-to-nature set.

good surfing in the area, and you can find charter boats for fishing and diving. The immediate area has some coral reefs, and the more adventurous can take trips to the Murciélago Islands to the north.

Although the town itself is a little on the grubby side, a short walk from the center will bring you to some **spectacularly beautiful beaches**, dotted with huge rocks and backdropped by lush mountains. Nearby, the smaller towns of **Ocotal** to the south, and **Playa Hermosa** and **Playa Panamá** to the north, are more secluded and laid-back, with equally lovely beaches. Farther south are Brasilito and Playa Flamingo.

Playa Flamingo
This is a beautiful white sand beach on a large horseshoe-shaped bay. It's not much of a town: most of the action centers around some new real estate developments. However, there are a couple of nice resorts and the marina offers the most extensive deep-sea fishing opportunities in the region.

Yellow Fin Sport Fishing is one of several outfits offering deep-sea fishing charters for sailfish, as well as scuba diving trips to the nearby Santa Catalina Island area. *Info: www.yellowfinsportfishing.com; Tel. 2653-9024, 8813 9675.*

Playa Potrero
Right next to Playa Flamingo, this is **one of the best beaches for swimming**, with very nice sand and mellow surf. If you are staying at the Paradisus Playa Conchal, this is a nice nearby beach to visit if you feel like getting out for an afternoon. The nicest part of the beach is near hotel Bahía del Sol. Drive north from Potrero via a bone-jarring dirt road to reach two isolated and beautiful spots, **Playa La Penca** and **Playa Pan de Azúcar**.

The town of Potrero itself is a typical small Costa Rican town but with condos and upscale developments cranking up in the nearby hills.

Playa Brasilito
This funky little beach town has a few budget lodgings and an especially nice swimming beach, with a nice expanse of grey sand. It's popular with Ticos and can get crowded on the weekends. The last time I was there the building boom had not yet started and the place was very quiet. Cross your fingers. You can walk here in just a few minutes from Paradisus Playa Conchal.

Playa Conchal
This beach, at the village of Puerto Viejo near Brasilito, is famous for its **beautiful white sand beach**, which is made up of tiny pieces of seashells. The beach is large, beautiful and never crowded, but strong currents make it dangerous for swimming.

This is where the prestigious all-inclusive **Paradisus Playa Conchal** is located, dominating the shoreline in front of the nicest part of the beach. Other than that, the village consists of little more than a few budget lodgings, but there are several boats offering fishing and diving charters. Divers love the abundance of rays and sharks. The same currents that make it dodgy for swimming make it a top surfing spot.

Tamarindo
Tamarindo is the largest town on the coast, such as it is. There is a "downtown" lined with tourist shops, restaurants, funky beach bars and hotels. Back streets hide more of the same. There is a festering surfer colony, and quite a few expats either retired or just going to seed in the tropics. You used to be able to see a couple of pigs roaming around, but those days are gone.

The beach always seems to be filled with surfers. The break is close in, so it's a good place to watch the experts.

There are some great places to stay, and several restaurants vie with each other for serving the most interesting Pacific Rim seafood fusions. Nightlife is young and laid-back. Ironically, occasional dragnets through the kitchens of local restaurants by immigration authorities yield a few young gringos working for bananas. They get shipped back home to the US at Daddy's expense.

The **new shopping mall i**n Tamarindo is worth a visit. It's in an upscale eco-friendly development, and has outdoor cafes and classy shops.

Perhaps not the hippest town in Costa Rica, Tamarindo is probably the most happening or lively spot in the Nicoya Peninsula. Good surf, great restaurants, plenty of nightlife choices and a wide variety of lodging choices all make it popular. It's also popular because of its popularity—the young crowd flocks here to hang out with the plentiful 20-somethings from all over the world. Tourists of all types enjoy the beaches, shopping and overall beach town atmosphere. I love the town even though there aren't any pigs running around in the streets anymore.

> ### No Lifeguard on Duty
> Many of the Pacific beaches feature thunderous surf and wildly picturesque rock formations. While surfing may be spectacular, **swimming can be risky**. At certain beaches, it's simply not safe. If swimming is your goal, look for someplace in a protected bay. Always check local conditions, stay close to shore, and be extremely cautious at isolated beaches far from towns.

Playa Junquillal

This tiny town has a large secluded beach. South of here, the beaches are stunning and almost deserted. The two-mile long beach has only a few hotels and restaurants. Surfing near the estuary mouth is the big deal. The surf can be quite rough for swimmers. This is a wonderful, wonderful beach for **long romantic walks**. You can wade across the mouth of the Rio Nandamojo at low tide and walk a couple more miles to Playa Lagarto. Look for crocs.

From July to January **olive Ridley** and **leatherback sea turtles** come ashore to nest.

Once past **Carrillo**, roads are interesting to say the least, with some dodgy river crossings. At some of these fords, you won't find your way safely across without local help, so be patient and seek detailed directions from the locals when you see them wading across.

Playa Ostional

Just north of Nosara, Ostional is famous for the vast hordes of **Ridley turtles** that pull in from July to November to lay their eggs. Even though the beach is 8 km long, the turtles insist on using only a small stretch of less than 1 km, and rarely lay eggs anywhere else. They prefer the last quarter of the moon to do their thing.

The **Ostional Wildlife Refuge** protects marine turtle species, such as the olive Ridley and leatherback. Mass turtle landings, *arribadas*, here may be the largest in the world, with as many as a million sea turtle eggs laid on the beach every year.

Sámara

I like Sámara. Long popular with Tico families as a weekend getaway, there is a nice selection of restaurants and bars. The beach is long and calm—usually good for swimming. Recently a small population of expats has grown and a real estate boom is either imminent or just passed. Hard to say. The town still has a nice beach atmosphere. The roads are all paved so it's easy to get to.

Area activities include kayaking, good snorkeling, scuba diving, fishing, boat tours, yoga and getting married. For some reason, this is a popular Tico wedding spot.

Playa Islita

Dominated by the superb **Punta Islita Lodge**, the beach is long and curving with rocky points at each end. Tourists race up and down on horses and the medium-size surf is popular with boogie boarders and beginning surfers. The hotel has a great pool and bar near the sand. The main part of the hotel is on a hill above the beach with a long walkway down to the beachside pool and bar. You can also go down via zip line.

This is one of the first places I would recommend for a romantic getaway in Costa Rica. The hotel is luxurious and intimate, with private plunge pools. The restaurant is one of the best on the coast. The beach is great and there are plenty of things to do in the area. The roads leading to the Playa Islita are rough, including one stretch where you have to ford a small river. The first time I drove through I forgot to roll up the driver's side window and I got soaked as the car plowed through the river with water halfway up the doors. But there is a small airport so you can skip all that if you like.

Mal País

If Montezuma is a hippie hangout, this is definitely a surfer town. There's not much here but a very cheap surfer lodging called **Mal País Surf Camp and Resort** (*www.malpaissurfcamp.com*), a few lodges, a couple of bars and the totally awesome break. Just outside town are even more beaches and some interesting places to stay. Cabo Blanco Preserve at the southern tip of the peninsula, is one of Costa Rica's finest parks.

Montezuma

This **secluded village**, at the end of a long and steep road, is famous around the world for its **hippie vibe**. Rastas, New Agers and hairy backpackers mingle in the town center. Street stalls sell beads and pipes. Vegetarian fare and lively bars are easy to find. The town is surrounded by especially lush forest, and has a nice beach and various picturesque waterfalls nearby. Fishing, diving and horseback riding tours are on offer.

Cabo Blanco Reserve

At the southern tip of the peninsula, this very wild and remote wilderness reserve is **one of Costa Rica's finest parks.** It has the distinction of being the first protected area in the country, established in 1963 thanks to the efforts of Swedish environmentalist Nicolas Wessberg. It was only recently opened for public visits.

The well-marked **Sueco Trail** is 4.5 km of ups and downs through luxuriant forest, finally leading to the beach, where you'll see the white (with seabird guano) cape that gives the park its name. The climate here is drier than in the uplands around Monteverde, with many evergreen trees. You'll see a vast variety of seabirds, and if you're patient, you may see white-tailed deer, anteaters, three kinds of monkeys, peccaries, coyotes, and maybe even signs of an ocelot.

The ranger station is two miles south of Cabuya (past Montezuma), on a poor road that may be impassable during the rainy season. You can get a taxi to the reserve, and also arrange for guided tours, in Montezuma. *Info: www.caboblancopark.com.*

Tambor

Down towards the southern end of the peninsula, the atmosphere is more laid-back, with **surfers** and **nature lovers** staying in budget lodgings, in contrast to the luxury resorts and big-buck fishing operations of the north.

Tambor is a quiet little town with a beautiful beach, quite good for swimming, and a few sleazy, colorful beach bars where locals and expats swap travel stories. I find little of interest in the town itself but there are some nearby attractions. Temptation Island II was filmed here and whales are said to come into the bay in large numbers.

Curú Wildlife Refuge

Curú National Wildlife Refuge and Hacienda is one of the smallest wildlife preserves in Costa Rica, but it has at least **five distinct ecosystems**, including both moist and dry coastal forests and mangrove swamps. Curú is actually a privately run venture that includes a farm dedicated to sustainable agriculture and several ongoing conservation projects.

The proprietors are working to reintroduce spider monkeys and scarlet macaws, formerly extinct in the Nicoya region. They also rehabilitate orphaned animals for eventual release into the wild. Beware the spider monkeys that lurk near the entrance—the naughty little beggars have been spoiled by too much contact with humans, and idly loll about, waiting for unsuspecting tourists to take advantage of.

There are 11 hiking trails of varying lengths and levels of difficulty, on which you may encounter forest dwellers such as three species of monkeys, peccaries, kinkajous, anteaters and coyotes. The preserve is also home to wild cats including ocelots, pumas, and margays, as well as over 230 species of birds. The beach is a nesting ground for several species of sea turtles, and the mangroves form an important habitat where many types of fish and other sea creatures spend part of their life cycles.

Curú's beach is perfect habitat not only for turtles, but for tourists as well, with a spectacular setting, nice sand and calm water that's safe for swimming. Horses are available for rent. Cheap lodging is available in some very basic cabins near the beach. *Info: Open daily 7am-3pm. Entrance: $8. www.curuwildliferefuge.com; Tel. 2641-0100.*

Gulf of Nicoya Islands

The Gulf of Nicoya has a host of islands of various sizes. Some have just a tiny village or two, and some are uninhabited by humans. All are absolutely teeming with birds. There are guided boat tours to several of the islands, and the hardy can visit by kayak.

The most popular is **Tortuga Island** (actually a pair of islands), just off-shore from Curú. You can easily book a day trip here from Puntarenas, but the islands are by no means overrun (yet). The beaches are exquisite, gently sloping white sand perfect for swimming and snorkeling, and there are no permanent inhabitants to disturb the animals and birds you'll see along the hiking trails.

At the mouth of the Gulf, **Guayabo** and the **Islas Negritos** are protected biological reserves. You can't go ashore, but avid birders can watch the action from a boat.

Chira, the largest island in the gulf, mostly consists of an enormous expanse of mangrove swamps and salt pans, frequented by flocks of wading birds and swarms of mosquitoes. A couple thousand locals cultivate oysters and gather salt. There are said to be a couple of budget lodgings on the island.

Venado, the second-largest island, also has some very basic accommodations and lots of bird-filled mangroves. You can take a tour here from Jicaral.

Other uninhabited or almost-uninhabited islands are **Isla Caballo**, which has some lovely beaches, and **Isla San Lucas**, a former penal colony with a very colorful history.

Santa Rosa National Park

Here at the northwestern corner of Costa Rica, the Nicaraguan border traverses a narrow strip of land between the Pacific Ocean and Lake Nicaragua. The region was destined by geography to be the site of several historic happenings. Santa Rosa National Park was established in 1971 to commemorate the site of the Battle of Santa Rosa, an 1856 battle in which Costa Rica fought off an invasion attempt by Nicaraguan troops allied to American adventurer William Walker. During the battle, a young man from Alajuela named **Juan Santamaría** became one of Costa Rica's national heroes when he bravely set fire to the Nicaraguans' stronghold, getting killed in the process.

Nicaraguan dictator Somoza made an abortive attack here in 1955. In the 1980s the CIA had a secret airstrip and a training camp for the Nicaraguan contras in what is now the Murciélago sector of the park.

This large (495 square km) coastal park is part of a network of parks in the region, called the Guanacaste Conservation Area. Santa Rosa contains at least **a dozen different habitats**, including deciduous forest, marshlands and mangrove swamps, as well as open scrub-dotted savannas, a legacy of former slash-and-burn agriculture.

Santa Rosa is an excellent place to observe wildlife, especially in the dry season, when animals come to drink at the few watering holes, and the comparatively open terrain makes the critters a little easier to spot. The park boasts 115 mammal species and 250 bird species. You're sure to spot

coatis (see photo at left), deer and a monkey or two (howler, spider, and capuchin varieties). Coyotes, tapirs and peccaries are a bit more elusive. If you're really lucky, you may see a wild cat: jaguars, pumas, ocelots, margays and jaguarundis all live in the park. The best trails for spotting animals are the short (1.5 km) **Naked Indian Trail** and the longer **Los Patos** and **Laguna Escondida trails**.

The park is easily accessible by road, with two ranger stations just off the Interamerican Highway. At the Santa Rosa Sector to the south you'll find **Hacienda Santa Rosa** (also known as La Casona), an old colonial plantation house where the famous battle of 1856 was fought. It's now a slightly interesting historical museum. Several hiking trails originate here.

Beaches in Santa Rosa

There are a couple of beautiful beaches in the park, which are very hard to get to, and therefore quite untouristed. **Playa Nancite** is one of a handful of nesting sites in the world for the endangered olive Ridley sea turtles, who visit from August through December. Humans wishing to visit must have a permit, which you can get from the ranger station.

Playa Naranjo and its **Witches Rock** are famous for quite a different reason. The long tubular break is a legend among surfers. There's little here but a very rustic camping area. There's a so-called road leading from Hacienda Santa Rosa to Nancite and Naranjo, but it's passable only with a 4WD vehicle, if at all.

There's another ranger station to the north, at the Murciélago sector, about 15 km from the highway. There's a camping area with restrooms and showers. The road is challenging, with several river crossings, but usually passable with a 4WD vehicle. It ends at **Playa Blanca**, an unbelievably beautiful white-sand beach frequented by pizotes and other local critters, but not by tourists. Always inquire about local road conditions, and keep your passport handy, as there are several police checkpoints in the area. South of here are several equally beautiful and even more isolated beaches, accessible only by boat.

The **Santa Elena Peninsula** is one of the few areas on the Pacific coast with extensive coral reefs. The most famous dive site is the **Islas Murciélagos** (Bat Islands), which is frequented by the gentle giants of the sea, filter-feeding whale sharks, as well as several much less cuddly species of shark. Advanced divers only, please. There's nothing on the islands but a small ranger station with very minimal camping facilities.

You can hire a local panga at the little fishing village of **Jobo** to visit the Bat Islands or any of the isolated beaches, but for dive charters, you'll have to go to Playa Flamingo, on the Nicoya Peninsula to the south.

The main ranger station is at the Santa Rosa Sector (take Highway One 37 km north from Liberia, then take a dirt road about 6 km). There's a camping area with restrooms and showers. *Info: Open daily 8am-4pm. Entry: $6. www.acguanacaste.ac.cr; Tel. 2666-5051.*

BEST SLEEPS & EATS
BEST SLEEPS IN PAPAGAYO
Four Seasons $$$$$
By itself at the very end of Punta Mala, across Bahía Culebra (Snake Bay), opposite Playas del Coco, Playa Hermosa and Playa Panama, this is one of the most luxurious places to stay in Nicoya. The **Arnold Palmer-designed golf course** is one of the top three in the country. There are three swimming pools, two tennis courts (one is a stadium court) and a tropically serene spa. Wireless internet access works over most of the property.

The cheapest rooms here go for over $400 a night and prices

rise to well over $2,000. The hotel has been experimenting with all-inclusive packages and currently offers a wide variety of deals involving one or more meals, spa, golf and "romance" credits.

Service is attentive. The beach is okay, but not spectacular. Still, this is a Four Seasons and that means pampering and top-quality service and amenities. Everything about the place is very expensive and I've recently heard reports of poor quality food.

You need a taxi to get anywhere from the hotel. Check on their child policy before booking. *Info: www.fourseasons.com/costarica; Tel. 2696-0000.*

Hilton Papagayo Resort $$$$
Formerly El Nakuti, Sol Papagayo also enjoys proximity to the wonderful **Playa Panama**. There is a large pool. Some of the rooms are in freestanding  villas. It would be a good idea to inquire about upgrading to one of their "executive suites." Be sure you specify a room with an ocean view. *Info: Playa Panama. www.hiltonpapagayoresort.com; Tel. 2672-0000.*

El Ocotal Beach Resort $$$
Diving central! Ocotal is perched high on a hill overlooking the spectacular bay around Playas del Coco. The view is truly awesome and earns the adjective "panoramic." Be sure you get one of the rooms facing the ocean, or your view will be merely ho-hum.

They have a **top-quality dive operation** right on the property. Fishing for sails and marlin is top-notch just offshore, in season. There always seems to be a troop of howler monkeys in the trees stirring things up. The beach is nice and they have a couple of good bars. The restaurant is nothing that great, but has a wonderful view. Rooms are in motel-style buildings and are quite pleasant, with all the goodies, including TVs, AC, phones and safes. *Info: South of Playas del Coco. www.ocotalresort.com; Tel. 2280-4976.*

Giardini de Papagayo $$$
An all-inclusive resort set on the hills just above Playa Panama, the Giardini has good views from most rooms and is convenient to the beach. The beach is sandy and good for swimming—no rocks. The rooms are in small villas with patios and are nicely furnished. There is a **large pool** with some shady areas. Staff can help arrange all types of activities. The **all-inclusive**

deals include room, meals, wine and drinks. *Info: Playa Panama. Tel. 2672-0067, 888/790-5264 US.*

BEST SLEEPS IN FLAMINGO
Paradisus Resort $$$$

Probably **the nicest all-inclusive resort in Costa Rica**, Playa Conchal has everything you need, and is quietly luxurious. Kids love the complicated, huge, tropically landscaped pool, one of the biggest in Latin America with

two kiddie pools and two Jacuzzis. The hamburgers and fries at the pool restaurant are definitely up to US standards. The eco-recreational Kid's Club keeps them out of your hair, so you can sip umbrella drinks and play golf. The program is designed to keep them eco-entertained with two playgrounds, mini climbing wall, mini disco, table games, movies, eco-recreational team, children's menu, and kidsize nap areas.

The **Robert Trent Jones golf course** suffers only slightly from **monkeys**. The green fee is a mere $125 with cart. There are four tennis courts, a casino and the obligatory onsite zip line canopy tour.

The three restaurants are of good quality, but nothing like some of the fine dining spots in the Central Valley. Breakfast buffets have the required omelet and pancake stations—something for the whole family.

Battery-powered shuttles roam the property carrying guests to and fro. The walled property fronts on Playa Conchal, which is really the only pure white beach in Costa Rica. The finely ground white shell beach, one of the nicest in the country, is good for swimming or wandering, and there is **decent snorkeling nearby**.

Although the resort provides everything you need and discourages trips outside the walls, this would be a good base for exploring the other beaches and attractions of the area. Condos with kitchens are available by the week. You can choose to go with the all-inclusive deal and eat in the resort, or eat your own cooking and visit nearby restaurants. There are a couple of nice seafood joints in the nearby village. *Info: Brasilito. www.paradisus. com/paradisus-playa-conchal.php; Tel. 888/741-5600 US.*

Flamingo Beach Resort $$

Playa Flamingo is directly in front of this place, so you can enjoy the **beach activities** and easily slip back to your room to freshen up. Ocean-view suites are the preferred rooms, as they are quieter than the pool-side rooms. The wonderful restaurant **Marie's** is just across the street. Of course there is a central pool with swim-up bar and lighted tennis courts. There are three restaurants with room service and two bars.

I have had reports of overbooking, so be sure to confirm well in advance and call or fax again a night or two before arriving. Check their web site or call for specials. *Info: Playa Flamingo. www.resortflamingobeach.com; Tel. 877/856-5519 US.*

BEST SLEEPS IN TAMARINDO

Hotel El Jardín del Edén $$$

Perched on the hill just behind town, the Edén boasts a panoramic vista of Tamarindo Bay, probably **the best view** of all the local hotels. The new French owners have made extensive upgrades to the property.

The 34 rooms are in five villas, and are individually isolated and reasonably private. All the rooms have AC, ceiling fans, TVs, phones, safes, hair dryers and balconies or patios. There are also two apartments with kitchens.

The pool and Jacuzzi are lovely, surrounded by green vegetation, with tropical umbrella drink "poolside services." The restaurant has **wonderful Italian food** and great views. It's a walk into town or to the beach, which is not so bad. The walk back up the hill however, is something to consider. *Info: www.jardindeleden.com; Tel. 2653-0137.*

Hotel Capitán Suizo $$$

Everyone loves this place, which is run by a Swiss couple. Right by one of the best parts of the beach, it is a little out of town, but that's not a bad

thing. It is one of the more luxurious properties in Tamarindo. Pool, restaurant and bar are pleasant and only a few steps from the beach. It is a member of **Small Distinctive Hotels of Costa Rica**.

The 22 rooms and 8 bungalows are very cheerful, with stone floors and whimsical colors on the walls. Amenities include phones, safes and refrigerators. Some rooms have AC. Sliding glass doors open onto patios or balconies. If you like sleeping with a cool tropical breeze, ask for one of the rooms on the upper floor. *Info: www.hotelcapitansuizo.com; Tel. 2653-0075.*

Villa Alegre $$$

One of the nicest B&Bs I have visited, Villa Alegre is well run by Barry and Suzye Lawson. It's just above the beach, Playa Langosta, with **good surfing** right in front. The wonderful sound of surf fills the air. You can walk to town along the beach. The owners are very friendly and are glad to help you find your way around. Barry is an avid golfer and knows all the pros in the area.

All the rooms are individually air-conditioned and have safes. A couple of fluffy dogs are available if needed. You are allowed to raid the refrigerator at night. There is a nice pool. This is one of the most pleasant of the few actual beachfront lodgings in Tamarindo. Villa Alegre is **one of my favorite places to stay**. *Info: www.villaalegrecostarica.com; Tel. 2653-0270.*

Hotel y Villas Cala Luna $$$

The villas at Cala Luna are **simply fantastic**. I love the stucco Pacific Rim architecture. The basic rooms are okay, but the villas with their **private plunge pools**, kitchens, etc. are isolated, quiet and special. Honeymooners love the privacy. They are nicely decorated and well furnished. They

come with full kitchens, laundry and everything you need to escape. The restaurant serves fresh seafood, pasta and steaks, but I find more interesting places to eat nearby. It is very nice but a little pricey for a place that's not directly on the beach (the beach is across the street and down a path). *Info: www.calaluna.com; Tel. 2653-0214, 800/210-0919 US.*

BEST SLEEPS SOUTH OF TAMARINDO

Hacienda Pinilla $$$

Hacienda Pinilla is a very large (4,500 acres) luxury residential development where you can purchase homes, beach villas and condos, or simply stay in opulence and enjoy the **Mike Young-designed golf course**. The luxurious, expensive resort has an abundance of everything that appeals to the up-market traveler.

Amenities include three miles of coastline, extensive stables and riding facilities, lighted tennis courts, and on and on. The Posada del Sol hotel, beach houses and Casa Golf Suites offer a variety of top quality options. They have interesting specials that can make Pinilla a reasonably priced option for luxury accommodations in the area.

The list of activities is endless. The staff arranges all manner of trips to local attractions and adventures. In spite of the snobby atmosphere, Pinilla

BEST OF THE BEST –
OUR FAVORITE LODGING IN THE
NORTH PACIFIC COAST
Hotel Punta Islita $$$$$

A member of the **Small Luxury Hotels of the World** group, this is **one of the best hotels in the country**. The views out to the Pacific from the rooms and from the infinity pool are spectacular. The beach is a short walk away, and is a **good swimming beach**. There is another pool with a bar by the beach, right at the edge of the sand.

Service is almost over the top—arriving guests are greeted with hot towels and refreshing fruit drinks. The cabinas are immaculate, luxurious and romantic with hammocks just big enough for two and very private plunge pools surrounded by exotic tropical vegetation with views out over the Pacific, also just big enough for two. This is a very good choice for a wedding venue. The hotel is, deservedly, very popular with honeymooners. It is isolated and quiet.

The **restaurant is one of the best on the coast**, heavy with seafood and with a good wine list, mostly Spanish and Chilean. The cabinas are romantic. In the evenings, the restaurant is thick with honeymooners mooning over their tables at each other with cow eyes.

The trip to the hotel by road is interesting. Make sure you call ahead to check on the tides, as a couple of the rivers you'll have to cross can get high. In the green season, portions of the road are almost impassable. **They have their own airport** with a good road to the hotel, so you can always get there. Call ahead. *Info: www.hotelpuntaislita.com; Tel. 2231-6122, 866/446-4053 US.*

is the sponsor of the annual Costa Rica-wide **Pinilla Classic National Surfing Championships**. Even hardcore twitchers won't be disappointed, with over 300 species of birds to choose from. *Info: www.haciendapinilla. com; Tel. 2680-3000, 866/294-0466 US.*

Guanamar $$$
With 40 air-conditioned rooms and suites with all the trimmings, Guanamar is a **fishing-oriented resort**. It is a little worn but otherwise comfortable. The rooms all have, safes, TVs and phones. Restaurant, bar and pool are nice with great views out to sea. Fish on the menu comes from local fishermen. This is one of the top fishing tournament locations in the country. The best fishing grounds are not very far offshore, so fishing time is maximized in this area. It is not unusual to hook 25 or 30 sailfish and a couple of marlin in one day. Guanamar is the place to make this kind of fishing action happen. *Info: www.guanamarhotel.com; Tel. 2656-0054.*

BEST SLEEPS IN MAL PAÍS
Hotel Flor Blanca $$$$$
With only ten separate stucco and tile villas, the Flor Blanca is one of the quietest, most **luxurious** and interesting places to stay in Costa Rica. Although the original developers have left the scene, the hotel continues to offer hip, upscale travelers deluxe beachfront digs. At $675 and up per night, one expects only the best linens, furniture and decorations. There's a New Age, Pac Rim atmosphere. Facilities include a two-level pool with waterfall, music room with piano, art studio, yoga/pilates studio, a dojo for karate and yoga, and a big Tai-chi scene.

The hotel is located in Santa Teresa on the dirt road leading north from Malpaís. The **surfing** in the area is legendary.

Their literature states that no children under the age of 13 are allowed, but their website has pictures of babies enjoying the pool with mummy. Maybe they make exceptions if you are the Kennedys, who are rumored to rent the whole place for weeks at a time.

I have heard reports that the level of service has deteriorated with the new owners. Some staff may have been hired for surfing ability and cool-ness rather than service attitude and hospitality experience. *Info: www. florblanca.com; Tel. 2640-0232.*

Avoid Bahía Luminosa

I no longer recommend the Hotel Bahía Luminosa. It used to be a beautiful property, but has become sadly run-down in the last few years. Rumors of new owners and a grand reopening remain just that: rumors.

BEST SLEEPS IN TAMBOR
Tambor Tropical $$$
The rooms are all large, beautiful suites with **imaginative and detailed woodwork**, full kitchens and all the goodies. The shady grounds front on the beach, but are also right in the village, so the beach is a little on the busy side and the hotel itself gets **noisy**. Most rooms face the bar and pool, which can be a problem, as the bar can get interesting (loud) as the night

wears on. There are plenty of shady hammocks. No kids. *Info: www.tambortropical. com; Tel. 2365-2872, 866/890-2537 US.*

Hotel Tango Mar $$$

This is a luxurious 150-acre resort with a **nine-hole golf course** fronting right on one of the most visually **spectacular beaches** in the country. The Belgian owners have recently remodeled all the rooms and public spaces. The villas are on a hill above the beach and have fantastic views out towards the Pacific. The Cristóbal restaurant features (of course) seafood, and is quite good.

The beach is amazing, with awesome surf and photogenic waterfalls. The TV show *Temptation Island* was filmed here. On-site are a pool and tennis courts (bring your own racket). There's not much else in the area, but Tambor, Montezuma and Malpaís are a short drive away. Great! *Info: www.tangomar.com; Tel. 2683-0001.*

El Sano Banano / Ylang Ylang Beach Resort $ / $$$

El Sano Banano Village Hotel (careful: there is a Sano Banano Hotel in Puntarenas that is not the same place) offers 12 basic but comfortable air-conditioned rooms above the restaurant of the same name, which has long been a favorite in Montezuma.

The same outfit operates the much more interesting (and much pricier) Ylang Ylang Beach Resort, which is on the beach about 15 minutes from

the village. There is no road to the hotel—you have to walk (the staff will bring your luggage). All by itself amid miles of unspoiled jungle, the resort features eight little cabins, some with outdoor garden showers, a waterfall pool and an outdoor restaurant— *muy romantico* by candlelight at night. This might be the secluded paradise we have all been looking for! *Info: www.elbanano.com; Tel. 2642-0636.*

Costa Coral $$
This 10-room hotel was completely renovated in 2009. It has lush gardens, a rooftop patio and a nice pool. The Canadian owners offer great hospitality. The restaurant has an international menu and a decent wine list. *Info: 100 meters from the Cemetery. www.hotelcostacoral.com; Tel. 2683-0105.*

BEST EATS IN FLAMINGO
Camarón Dorado $$$
Local sport-fishing captain Jorge Segueira runs **the best place to eat** for miles around in Brasilito. It's usually packed. Tourists love the simply prepared and well-presented **seafood**, right on the beach with the breeze blowing through. It's a little pricey but worth a splurge. Very romantic. *Info: Tel. 2654-4028.*

Marie's Restaurant $$
On the plaza in Playa Flamingo, Marie's has no particular view or anything, but it does have good food and a nice atmosphere. **Grand fish sandwiches**. The juice drips off your elbow as you bite into them. I like to order the whole snapper. *Info: www.mariesrestaurantincostarica.com.*

BEST EATS IN TAMARINDO
Gecko's $$
In the Iguana Surf Shop, Gecko's does a good job, with **great seafood** for breakfast, lunch and dinner. You can eat great hunks of mahi and tuna.

Happy Snapper $$
Everybody seems to like the Happy Snapper in Brasilito, with its lively bar

---

Costa Rican Riviera
The **Nicoya Peninsula is experiencing a boom** in tourist traffic and development. Huge resort hotel projects are underway or are being planned. With the airport in Liberia now handling 15 to 20 flights from North America daily, eating and sleeping options are quite varied and growing. In most areas, the best eating is at the restaurants of the lodges and hotels. A few towns like **Tamarindo** are big enough to offer a choice of interesting restaurants. Eating roast fish and drinking beer in thatched huts by the water is definitely on.

and good-quality local specialties. It's a bit of a hangout with live music on the weekends. *Info: Tel. 2654-4413.*

BEST EATS IN TAMBOR, MONTEZUMA, MAL PAÍS
Pancho's $$$
On the water at the edge of Tambor, over by the fishermen's dock and the yacht club, is Pancho's, with some of **the freshest seafood** you'll ever find. It's **not cheap** ($45 for a lobster!) after being inundated by the big-spending production staff of the TV show *Temptation Island* for months of shooting. The service is good. The dogs are friendly but usually asleep. *Info: On the edge of Tambor.*

Sano Banano $$
Right in the middle of Montezuma is the popular Sano Banano, famous for **banana pancakes** and *pargo entero* (whole red snapper). You have to eat here at least once. Try to get a seat with a view of the street action, such as it is. They show dubious movies after dinner. *Info: Tel. 2642-0636.*

BEST SHOPPING
Tamarindo
With European designer clothing and accessories, **Bamboo Groove** is probably the most upscale shopping experience in town. *Info: Plaza Tamarindo.*

Guaitíl
Guaitíl is one of the few really **world-class craft** centers in Costa Rica. The people of the village take advantage of local clay deposits to make a variety of pottery. Nice pots and other ceramic items feature themes from the mythology of the **indigenous Chorotegas people**, including stylized jaguars, toucans, and the Chorotegas Fire God, a sort of snake with feathers. You can watch native potters at work and, of course, buy their attractive designs and even have them shipped back to the US. Women run most of the potteries. *Info: Guaitíl is easy enough to get to, about 12 km off the main highway, past the town of Santa Barbara.*

BEST SPORTS & RECREATION
BOATING, CRUISES
Calypso Cruises
Operating out of Puntarenas, **Calypso Cruises** offers day trips to Tortuga Island and Punta Coral Private Reserve including transportation from San

José and Jacó on a roomy catamaran. Trips include breakfast, lunch with wine and live music. Snorkeling equipment is provided on the Coral Preserve cruise. *Info: www.calypsocruises.com; Tel. 2256-2727.*

Seascape Kayak Tours

Seascape Kayak Tours, in Tambor, offers trips to the nearby Curú Wildlife Refuge from October through May. *Info: www.seascapekayaktours.com; Tel. 8314-8605.*

FISHING
Playa Coco

Alonso Lara runs a 25-footer with a four-stroke Suzuki engine, and supplies Shimano tackle. You might want to bring light tackle of your own. Expect to fish offshore and at Bat Island in Santa Rosa National Park with lures and live bait. *Info: $380 all day. Tel. 2820-4912.*

Calypso Cruises (see information above) also offers sport fishing trips.

SCUBA DIVING/SNORKELING
Tamarindo

Agua Rica Diving Center takes divers to Islas Catalinas and other hot spots. Resort course and night dives are available. *Info: Info: www.tamarindo.com/agua; Tel. 2653-0094.*

Ocotal

Ocotal Beach Marina operates just outside Coco in the Ocotal Resort. These are the guys to go with if you want to swim with the manta rays or get gobbled up by bull sharks. *Info: www.ocotalresort.com; Tel. 2280-4976.*

GOLF

In the 1990s, a parade of famous designers built several excellent oceanfront courses on the Nicoya Peninsula: **Garra de Leon**, at the lavish Paradisus Playa Conchal resort, is a 7,030-yard course that was designed by

Robert Trent Jones II. Watch the monkeys—they may steal your balls. Just down the coast are **Hacienda Pinilla Golf & Country Club**, a 7,274-yard Mike Young design, the **Royal Pacific Golf & Country Club** (6,802 yards, Ron Garl), and **Los Sueños**. At the resort of the same name, this 6,707-yard course was designed by Ted Robinson. This glamorous resort is also home to big-bucks fishing tournaments.

HORSEBACK RIDING

Haven't you always wanted to ride a horse on a beautiful tropical beach? Playa Conchal is the main place to go horseback riding here (see photo below). Set up an excursion from your hotel or try **Tamarindo Dreamers Adventure**. *Info: www.tamarindodreamersadventure.com; Tel. 8771-2373.*

9. THE CENTRAL PACIFIC COAST

Between the Nicoya Peninsula to the north and the Osa Peninsula to the south are some of Costa Rica's most frequented beach areas, including the country's two largest resort areas: **Jacó** and **Manuel Antonio**. However, secluded strands are not hard to find.

- **Crocodiles in the river at Tárcoles** – They're hanging out for all to see.

- **Fishing off Quepos** – It's Costa Rica's largest sport fishing center.

- **Manuel Antonio National Park** – It's worth braving the tourist hordes.

COORDINATES

This section of Costa Rica's Pacific coastline runs from Puntarenas to Palmar Norte. It is backed by spectacular mountains lush with tropical forests.

ONE GREAT DAY ON THE CENTRAL PACIFIC COAST

Both Jacó and Manuel Antonio are good spots for a day out. Both have great beaches and cool bars/restaurants to hang out in. And of course Manuel Antonio has **Manuel Antonio National Park**, packed with sloths and monkeys throwing turds at tourists. **Jacó** is two or more hours from San José and Manuel Antonio is another hour and a half further down the road.

With just one day, your best bet is either to head for one of the **great beach towns** described later in this chapter, or to visit **Carara National Park**, especially if you enjoy bird watching. However, be aware that this park, easy to get to from the capital, gets very crowded.

Morning

Coming down from San José, the road descends steeply to the palm-studded coast with spectacular views out over the Pacific. Shortly before reaching the coast, you'll cross a bridge at **Tárcoles**. The river below is stiff with crocodiles! Even if you're just passing through, do stop and have a quick look. Park on the side, give a little kid a buck to watch your car, walk out onto the bridge and join the parade of tourists observing the somnolent saurians.

There's a gift shop just before the bridge and usually a few people selling water coconuts (*pipas*). Vendors will slice the tops off the coconuts for you with a machete. Poke in a straw and enjoy! They are quite refreshing. You

can usually buy mangos, watermelons, papayas and pineapples here. Try some of each.

If you'd like a longer look at the famous croc population of the Tárcoles River, take a **Jungle Crocodile Safari**. Two-hour and half-day trips in a covered launch get you right up close to the big boys (plus lots of birds).

Afternoon

Near the coast, **Carara National Park** is easy to visit on a day trip from San José. The downside of its easy accessibility is predictable: it's almost always mobbed with tourists, including cruise ship passengers bused in for day trips. If you have more time to spare, skip this one.

Carara is **a favorite of birders**. Located in a transition zone between the Pacific rain forest ecosystem and the drier habitats to the north, the park has a particularly rich roster of bird species. The comparatively open woodland makes birds easier to spot than in the dense rain forest.

The park is thick with scarlet macaws, and you may also spot toucans, aracaris, tinamous, and all sorts of herons, anhingas, egrets and other water birds. You will certainly see many examples of the North American Twitcher, which may be almost as interesting to watch as the birdies.

The **Quebrada Bonita** ranger station and park headquarters is two miles south of the bridge over the Tárcoles River. There are two short hiking trails, each a little less than a mile long. Buses from San José stop at the station. No lodging or camping is available in the park. *Info: Entrance fee is $8. Hours are 8am-4pm.*

Evening

Head back with a carload of tired kids and a trunk full of wet clothes. It's a long drive back to San José. If you are staying closer, you have several choices of good restaurants to stop at on your way back. I like **Pacific Bistro** in Jacó and **El Gran Escape** in Quepos.

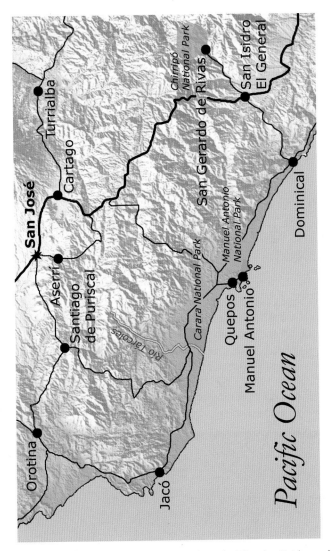

You can always stop again on your way back at the Tárcoles Bridge to look at the crocs that congregate there. Kids love it but keep a good hold on them.

A FANTASTIC WEEKEND ON THE CENTRAL PACIFIC COAST
If you'd like a lively beach town with lots of young people and a hopping nightlife scene, stay near Jacó. If you'd prefer a quieter, more upscale resort

area, stay around Manuel Antonio. Both places have excellent beaches, and both provide easy access to the wildlife wonders of **Manuel Antonio National Park** and the world-class sport-fishing fleet in nearby Quepos.

Jacó is a good place to base yourself for a weekend, but it is popular, and that means lots of people. If you love the beach, but can't stand the crowds at Jacó, no problem. Between Jacó and **Quepos/Manuel Antonio** are a lot of pretty little beaches, mostly deserted. Some have cabinas to stay in, and little restaurants. Both towns are known for nightlife. Nightlife in Jacó has a seedier reputation.

Friday

Playa Jacó is the biggest and most visited beach town in the country, popular with Ticos, tourists, beach bums, surfers and anglers, offering every kind of watery activity you could wish. It's within easy weekend-trip range of San José. This is the place to go if you want a lively beach town that's squarely on the beaten path.

Since it is the closest beach action to San José, Jacó has become quite popular with young Ticos out for a good time surfing, drinking and strutting their stuff up and down the beach. Over the last few years it has become a booming beach town with a "strip" packed with cheesy souvenir shops, loud bars and surfboard stores.

Construction cranes are starting to tower over town as the inevitable condos spring up. There are numerous Internet cafes, a head shop, a sex shop,

tattoo parlors and all the usual stuff found in any beach town in the world. US fast-food joints are out in force. I like the place, but the more mature crowd usually prefers Manuel Antonio a few miles south, or Tamarindo on the Nicoya Peninsula.

Hotel Club Del Mar is right on the beach at the quiet end of town. They have a nice pool and a good break directly in front of the hotel.

Saturday

Split Jacó early in the morning and enjoy the scenic drive to **Manuel Antonio**. I like to stop frequently on this route at some of the great viewpoints. Just outside Jacó is a good place for photos. You can see the Nicoya Peninsula on a clear day. I have seen whales blowing from some of these spots.

Manuel Antonio has plenty of accommodation choices, including some of the most luxurious and interesting lodging in the country. **La Mansión** is my favorite in Costa Rica.

Good eating is another feature of Manuel Antonio. Several of the hotels have top quality restaurants and the funky beachside **Mar y Sombra** is a fine spot for beer and fish (and rockin' out later in the evening). Check out the lobster buffet at the **Parador**.

Saturday Night

There are several hot spots in Manuel Antonio catering to a young crowd that likes to dance, dance, dance. **Mar y Sombra** on the beach near the entrance to the park cranks up after 10pm or so. If you can handle a small, cheesy casino, check out **Byblos** on Monday for ladies night. They have tropical dance night on Thursday and live music on Fridays. **Bambu Jam** has live music on Tuesdays and sometimes Fridays. **Barba Roja** sometimes has weekend jam sessions.

Sunday

It's a pretty long haul back to San José, but there are several good places to stop along the way and make a day out of it.

There's a variety of small roads heading off from the main highway, many of which lead to the beach. In some areas there are a couple of miles of sandy roads running along the beach passing by small fishing villages and weekend beach villas. I have found some nice, quiet beaches this way. It pays to poke around and explore some of the back roads.

Just to the south of Jacó, on the main road, there is **a woodworkers shop** on the right run by Eugenio who makes wonderful furniture out of exotic woods. This is a unique stop. His quirky creations are shipped to customers all over the world.

Don't forget the **crocodiles** at Tárcoles bridge. It just takes a few minutes to stop and gawk at them. Where else can you safely get so close to a dozen or so huge crocs?

ONE WEEK ON THE CENTRAL PACIFIC COAST

With a week, you can explore some great beaches in this area and still venture farther afield, hanging out in **Quepos** and visiting **Manuel Antonio National Park**, **Dominical** (only if you surf, otherwise give it a miss) and the other nearby national parks: **Ballena** and **Chirripó**.

Fishing along the coast for billfish and dorado (mahi) is some of the best in the world. Small, secluded beaches are dotted up and down the coast. Whales and dolphins frolic just offshore.

Two cool beach towns and half a dozen small surfer villages dot the coast.

Jacó

The beach itself is great, fine for swimming, surfing, tanning or just sitting at a bar and watching the young ladies strutting about in their bikinis and the young men playing soccer.

There are several nice resorts around Jacó. My favorite is the **Hotel Club Del Mar**, right on the beach at the quiet end of town.

And speaking of hotels in town: most stink. They're generally cheap and dirty, with surfers camping in the parking lot. The noisy strip through town is annoying, lined with t-shirt shops and seemingly hundreds of places hustling half-day tours to Monteverde (not practical) and over-priced fishing trips in leaky local *pangas*.

Tacky bars heave with dubious ladies of the night and dreadlocked, grungy North Americans offer drugs. The tourist restaurants are overpriced.

The beautiful beach is thronged with young, sexy surfers doing their thing like some sort of exotic seals. They won't bother you. You can avoid the noise and crap easily enough. You can sit in a bar and gaze out over all this while sipping a Bavaria Negra. Know what to avoid and the place can be lots of fun. I love the town.

Quepos

Right next to Manuel Antonio, Quepos is a typically grubby little port town, but it happens to be **the biggest sport-fishing center in the country**. If your goal is to catch a billfish, you'll have no problem finding a charter boat here. You can sleep, eat and party in one of the upscale places in Manuel Antonio, right next to Quepos. But don't miss **El Gran Escape** in Quepos for gigantic fish sandwiches, burgers and beer.

Manuel Antonio

This is not much of a town, but rather a strip leading from Quepos to the park, lined with hotels, restaurants, bars and tour operators. The road winds around the side of the mountain with views out to sea. Look closely and you might see sloths hanging around on power lines.

Compared to Jacó, Manuel Antonio attracts an older, more affluent crowd. There are more big-buck hotels here than anywhere else in Costa Rica. There are a couple of wonderful beaches, great for swimming, but the hotels are near the beach, rather than right on the beach.

Manuel Antonio National Park

Established in 1972, Manuel Antonio is the smallest (1,624 hectares) but most visited national park in the country. The vast flocks of tourists are such that **some days they admit no more visitors after late morning**.

There's a variety of hiking trails, winding along the beaches and through the forest. Most are not very well marked. There are 109 species of mammals and 184 of birds in the park. **Manuel Antonio** is one of the best places to see sloths (the Spanish name is *perezoso*, which simply means "lazy"), both two- and three-toed.

Manuel Antonio is one of the few places where you're likely to see the tiny squirrel monkey (*mono tití*). You're also likely to see white-faced and howler monkeys, agoutis, *pizotes*, opossums and iguanas. The forests are home to lots of scarlet macaws and toucans, and the coast has vast flocks of sea birds, such as pelicans, frigate birds and anhingas.

The beaches in the park are beautiful and pristine, from **Espadilla** in the north, to Manuel Antonio beach, the best for swimming, to **Third Beach** with its tidal pools, to the secluded **Puerto Escondido** in the south. *Info: Open Tue-Sun 7am-4pm. Entrance fee $10. www.manuelantoniopark.com is a privately-operated web site with links to various tour operators and lodging in the area. Tel. 2777-2100.*

Dominical
From Quepos south to Dominical, the road is particularly bad, passing through massive palm oil plantations. After that you'll meet up with the route coming down from San Isidro. The road from here on south was excellent a few years ago, when it was built. Alas, it hasn't been properly maintained, and now there are potholes that could swallow a whale shark.

Dominical is a dirty and unpaved town, with a lot of construction going on. It seems random and unplanned, with garbage piles next to restaurants, and trenches carrying septic wastes snaking through the village.

There's a highly colorful surfer scene going on. The beach at Dominical is great for surfing, but dangerous for swimming. The beaches to the south are super and only lightly touristed.

Restaurants include unclean places with terrible food and several blaring sports bars. I try not to eat in Dominical if possible, but there are a few places attempting tropical macrobiotic/Pac Rim/Marin County/fusion things with organic mango sauce at high prices.

Ballena National Marine Park

South of Dominical is **Ballena National Marine Park**, which was created to protect the coral reefs, and the humpback whales that congregate offshore from December through May (the name *ballena* means "whale"). Most of the park is underwater, but it includes a couple of stunningly beautiful beaches, **Playas Ballena** and **Uvita**, that are easily accessible from the coast road.

There are no park facilities to speak of, and little to see from shore other than the wonderful beaches. The beaches are excellent for strolling around on, especially at low tide when you can walk way out on the rocks. You can charter a boat from Dominical to snorkel the reefs, or hang out with the whales when they're around. *Info: The ranger station is near Rancho La Merced Wildlife Refuge, just north of Ballena, and is open 8am-4pm.*

Chirripó National Park

On the slopes of Cerro Chirripó, Costa Rica's highest mountain (12,530 feet), **Chirripó National Park** encompasses several different habitats within a difference in elevation of over 8,000 feet. Cloud and rain forest give way to sparse high-altitude landscape called *paramo*, or "wet desert."

Climbing all the way to the peak is not for the casual visitor. Although no technical mountain-climbing skills are required, it's a steep 30-mile round trip, with rain a virtual certainty, and temperatures that can be be-

low freezing in winter. Most climbers make the trip over three days, stopping to camp at Valle de los Crestones (which has bunk beds, a cooking area, and cold showers), about halfway up. If you reach the top, you'll have a spectacular view of both oceans and Costa Rica's mountain backbone.

You don't have to make the three-day trek to the summit to enjoy Chirripó. Shorter hikes from **San Gerardo de Rivas**, the gateway to the park, are quite feasible. There are a couple of low-priced lodges in town.

The climate up here is exquisite. Tropical vegetation from mangos to coconuts is as lush as you please, but the air is pleasantly cool. *Info: Take the Interamerican Highway to San Isidro de El General, then take a smaller road north to Rivas, then San Gerardo de Rivas. Entry $20. Tel. 2771-4582.*

BEST SLEEPS & EATS
BEST SLEEPS IN JACÓ
Los Sueños Marriott Ocean and Golf Resort $$$$
Probably **the snazziest lodging in the area**, Los Sueños seems to have it all. Once you are within the gates of this US-style development you'd never know if you were in Florida, California, or wherever. A **Ted Robinson-designed golf course** sets the tone for the whole place. The huge **marina** with its big-buck yachts is the largest in Central America, and is home to various fishing tournaments and some of the best captains in Costa Rica. It hosts large yachts for celebrities such as George Strait.

This is a luxury hotel with six restaurants, casino, bars, deluxe rooms and suites and business-service amenities. The best of their restaurants, **La Vista**, is one of the finest on the coast. Their **seafood buffet** with lobster is legendary. The only drawback is the beach. It is dirty gravel and simply not very appealing. The pool is elaborate and almost makes up for the lousy beach. *Info: Playa Herradura, just north of Jacó. www.lossuenosresort.com; Tel. 2630-4000, 866/865-9759 US.*

Villas Caletas $$$$

Perched on a hill with a **breathtaking view** of the sea and sky, Villas Caletas is another very good option for the luxury traveler. It's close to Jacó, with all the dubious pleasures of that beach town, but secluded and quiet. **Wedding parties and honeymooners** make up a significant part of their clientele. It is a member of Small Distinctive Hotels of Costa Rica. This resort is aimed squarely at up-market, jaded travelers. There are only 31 rooms, of which 14 are

stand-alone villas and 11 are suites. The elaborate décor is in an Italianate Art Deco style. Every luxury amenity is here, including nice touches such as bathrobes, umbrellas and little bottles of designer goo in the bathrooms. There are two restaurants and a bar. French-influenced cuisine is served in the formal El Mirador, or outdoors in a faux Greek amphitheatre overlooking the ocean. *Info: www.hotelvillacaletas.com; Tel. 2630-3000.*

Rowdy Beach Town

If the nightlife and beach-town scene keep you awake at night, **consider staying outside Jacó** and coming into town only when you need a bar, restaurant or t-shirt shop, or just feel like looking at the girls on the beach. **Most of the lodging in town**, except for the Hotel Club del Mar, **is at the lower end of the quality scale.** However, it's a young town, and most visitors come specifically to be close to the loud and rowdy beach town scene (in contrast to the advice I give here). Just realize that there are options if you are looking for a more luxurious and comfortable place to stay in the area.

Hotel Punta Leona $$$

Located only 62 miles from San José, Hotel Punta Leona is an all-inclusive 750-acre resort that seems to have everything. Popular with vacationing Tico families and Europeans, the resort is dwarfed by the enormous forest fronting on the Pacific by impressive Punta Leona (Lion Point). The two-

BEST OF THE BEST –
OUR FAVORITE LODGING IN THE JACÓ
AREA
Hotel Club Del Mar $$$

Former star of the Kansas City Chiefs, Ed Podolak was responsible for the complete renovation and reopening of the now-luxurious Hotel Club del Mar. Located on 2 1/2 acres just above the beach on the south end of Jacó, the hotel is without doubt the nicest place to stay in town. In fact, it's really the only hotel I can recommend in Jacó, and I recommend it wholeheartedly. If you are looking for a **palm-shaded beach vacation** with some restaurants and shopping nearby, this is the place. Hotel Club Del Mar lets you enjoy the funky beach town while wallowing in luxury nearby.

There are a few hotel-style rooms, but the best ones are the freestanding condos they rent, most of which have two bedrooms and come completely furnished with everything you need, including full kitchens and **washer/dryers**. The beds are king-size. The AC is ice cold. They have TVs with cable, phones, too many towels and all the expected luxury goodies. A couple of the rooms experience some noise from trucks coming down the hill, so request one close to the beach.

Everything is right in the palm trees at the top of the beach. You can surf in front of the rooms just past the pool. **Surf and boogie boards are available** at the front desk. Internet access is free and you can use your wireless laptop anywhere around the lobby, restaurant or pool.

The restaurant may seem a little expensive, but they serve good food and are a little cleaner and nicer than the ones in town. They usually have some mid-quality combo or solo artist entertaining in the bar/restaurant in the evenings. *Info: www.clubdelmarcostarica.com; Tel. 2634-3194, 866/978-5669 US.*

mile long brick driveway leads through bamboo thickets to a complete vacation destination. There are four restaurants, three bars, a disco, miniature golf, grocery store, gift shop, post office, telephone and internet center, three pools, real estate sales office, conference rooms, laundry, tennis courts, play ground, first aid station, business center and much more.

On-site zip lines, kayaking, butterfly farm, guided walks and a long list of activities for adults as well as full animation services for kids keeps guests occupied. The chalets are nicely furnished, air conditioned and comfortable and are favored by the numerous European guests who come for all-inclusive two-week stays. *Pizotes*, *mapaches* and scarlet macaws haunt the grounds. The property was built and is owned by Costa Ricans. Dozens of luxury homes have been built and seemingly hundreds more are under construction.

The restaurants feature typical Costa Rican tourist fare including dorado, shrimp, steaks and pasta. The $15 buffet at the Carabelas Restaurant is fine, although the lighting in the thatched structure is harsh and Latin music blares loudly at breakfast, lunch and dinner. The bars are pleasant, especially the one by the pool. *Info: Off the main highway between Tárcoles and Jacó. www.hotelpuntaleona.com; Tel. 2587-1000.*

The Captain's Lair $$$
The Captain's Lair is a group of six shaded casitas around a nice pool at the base of the hills covered in secondary forest convenient to Jacó and the charter boat docks at Los Sueños. If you are in the area for fishing, this is a good alternative to hotel living. Each casita has two bedrooms and a completely outfitted kitchen. All are air conditioned and modern with nice furniture, TVs and king-sized beds.

There is a small restaurant bar by the pool in case you don't feel like cooking. Owners Tom and Tatiana Carton live next door and keep things nice. Tom is one of the premier charter captains in Costa Rica and knows what his clients need after fishing. *Info: Herradura, just outside Jacó. www.captaintoms.com/Lodging; Tel. 2637-8994, 2393-5598.*

BEST SLEEPS IN MANUEL ANTONIO
Gaia Hotel and Reserve $$$$$
Miami Beach meets the tropics at this member of **Small Luxury Hotels of the World**. The contemporary white stucco and stainless steel creation

somehow blends stark modernism with tropical beauty into one of the finest hotel properties in the country. Set on 14 acres, part of which has been set aside as a reserve, the hotel soars above the coastline, offering some of the most spectacular views in a town that has so many spectacular views of the rocky shore and sandy beaches that superlatives crowd each other out in the competition.

This is a luxury hotel with everything: multi-tiered infinity pool, top-quality restaurant, 24/7 room service, bars with fancy tropical drinks, free transportation to and from airport and beach, in-room spa service, wireless internet, valet service, on-staff nature guides, yoga platform, handicapped trails and only 20 rooms served by over 75 staff. Rooms are almost futuristic with flat-screen TVs, portable phones, Italian bathroom fixtures, Balinese screens, original art on the walls, extremely fluffy king-sized beds, wood and Italian slate floors, Jacuzzis in all rooms, very private balconies, and on and on. No children under 16 are allowed. Like all the other hotels in town, it is perched on a hill with a helluva view.

The hotel restaurant, **La Luna,** is one of the finest dining rooms in Manuel Antonio. The menu leans heavily toward seafood from around the world with salmon, Chilean sea bass and the obligatory US Angus filet mignon. Expect dishes prepared with chipotle, prosciutto, ginger, grain mustard and roasted sesame vinaigrette. Service is spot on. The room has mild views of the private preserve. The wine list is impressive, and fancy coffee drinks stretch the imagination. *Info: www.gaiahr.com; Tel. 2777-9797, 800/226-2515 US.*

BEST OF THE BEST –
OUR FAVORITE LODGING IN ALL OF
COSTA RICA!
La Mansión $$$$

Luxury travel boffins have pronounced La Mansión to be **the best hotel in Costa Rica**, and few can dispute the claim. If you can get in, you are pampered and spoiled with **a staff ratio of well over 1 to 1**. It's quiet and seems small. International celebrities and diplomats lease the whole place for themselves and their retinues from time to time. There's plenty of room for bodyguards and nannies.

Although it can be a little hard to get a reservation during the high season, you should definitely call or e-mail to see if there are any specials available. Sometimes you can get a nice room here for a special price and live in luxury for a few days. It is certainly intimate enough to make a wonderful honeymoon spot. You can easily pop in for a visit to the foggy Bat Cave bar. They have a good choice of wines by the glass.

The **restaurant is outstanding**. The wines are from the owner's own wine cellar. The views over the beaches and bays to the Pacific are stupendous. Monkeys and sloths visit the pool. The hippest beach in town is nearby. *Info: www.lamansioninn.com; Tel. 2777-3489, 800/360-2071 US.*

include tennis courts, spa services, infinity swimming pool, and special event rooms. *Info: www.hotelparador.com; Tel. 2777-1414, 877/506-1414 US.*

BEST SLEEPS IN QUEPOS
Condotel Las Cascadas $$
This homey place has some charming condos and suites (from one to four bedrooms) on the edge of Quepos in a quiet residential area. All have kitchens, AC and patios, and most have ocean views. Monkeys and birds spy on you as you lounge in the pool. *Info: www.condotel-lascascadas.com; Tel. 888/800-8929 US.*

BEST SLEEPS IN CHIRRIPÓ
Trogon Lodge $
The Trogon Lodge is probably the most beautiful tropical lodge I have seen anywhere. It is set at the base of the cloud forest, and surrounded by acres and acres of highly manicured landscaping with thousands of flowers and exotic shrubs. Hummingbirds, quetzals, and trogons flit about. Trout ponds provide wonderful eating in the restaurant.

Visitors enjoy walks and a zip line through the nearby cloud forest. Personalized tours of the cloud forest are offered on foot or horseback. This is one of the most desired destinations for birders in the world. These tours are as unlike the Monteverde and Arenal tours as you can get. The area is quiet. This is the only lodge for miles around. There are no t-shirt shops or youths zooming around on four-wheelers with their hats on backwards. If you came to Costa Rica to see nature, this should be one of your first destination choices.

The rooms are not luxurious but are quite comfortable and clean. The lodge is waaay up in the mountains and it gets quite chilly. The rooms have heaters. You'll need a jacket. This would be a good overnight (or more) stopping point when driving from San José to the southern Pacific area. The same company operates the beachfront Mawamba Lodge in Tortuguero. *Info: San Gerardo de Dota, near Cerro de la Muerte. www.trogonlodge.com; Tel. 2293-8181.*

BEST EATS IN JACÓ
Pacific Bistro $$$$
Right on the strip, the Pacific serves dinner only. The chef prepares the most interesting food in town, an imaginative **California fusion** of Indonesian, Japanese, Thai and Continental dishes utilizing the best of local ingredients. Tuna comes in huge chunks. I suggest calling ahead to reserve a table near the street. The **friendly gringo owner** keeps the street hustlers away.

Poseidon $$$$
The Poseidon is highly recommended by many of the upscale hotels in the area and the food is good. Huge portions of tuna with wasabi, kim chee and balsamic vinaigrette, and imported steaks are offered. Their tuna is justifiably famous.

I'm not a fan for several reasons. The times I have eaten there, a wide variety of street vendors came by, hugged the staff and then proceeded to hover over the diners offering beads, coconut carvings, trinkets woven from palm fronds. One guy continuously tweeted three notes on a sweet potato while standing right behind me while I was eating. I realize this is sometimes an unavoidable part of the tourist dining experience but when I eat, especially expensively, I want to be left alone. My experience is that most of the other upscale eateries in town keep these types strictly outside. It was obvious that the staff knew these guys and welcomed their presence.

During one visit to the restaurant, a young man drove his smoke belching motorcycle almost into the restaurant itself to chat with the staff while he sat on the loudly running bike gunning the engine. Smoke and noise filled the dining room while they socialized.

Some of the tables are near the open grill and you can watch the cook as she prepares the food. A table nearer the back would be better for several reasons. I observed the cook using her bare hands to place raw chicken on the grill and then sprinkle sesame seeds over a dish ready to be taken to a diner. This is asking for an experience with salmonella.

After the owner complained about this negative review as it appeared in an earlier edition of this book, I made sure to visit again and found the situation to be much the same. The owner told me he runs a tight operation and that "I am in the restaurant four nights a week!" That's the problem right there: the owner is only in the place for four dinners a week out of 21 mealtimes. *Info: Calle Bohio. Tel. 2643-1642.*

Colonial $$$

One of the nicer places on the strip, the Colonial is open-air with a great view of the passing parade. Service is snappy and the food is excellent. Whole snapper, snook with mango sauce, sea bass, burgers and pasta are great. Strolling musicians hustling tips and street urchins selling pencils can be a problem here but the food is good. My companion liked the **snook with mango sauce**. I liked the snapper. *Info: On the main street in Jacó. Tel. 2643-3332.*

Pancho Villa's $$$

This Mexican eatery serves enchiladas and tacos, steaks and lobster and a castle of shrimp. The seats near the street are good for people watching. Do not go into the "nightclub" upstairs unless you are looking for sleazy hookers hustling over-priced umbrella drinks. *Info: On the strip.*

Marisquería el Hicaco $$$

This open-air place right by the beach is a fine spot to gobble big piles of **reasonably priced seafood**. Wednesday lobster night is famous. Some of the tables have a view of the beach action.

El Bohío $$

El Bohío is a crummy little beach bar and restaurant with a view of the beach where all sorts of surfing and skimpy bathing suit strutting is going on, right in front. You can lean on the rail sipping a beer on ice, taking in the scene while stuffing your face with whole fish, regular old bar-food, sandwiches, shrimp, etc. It's **a happenin' spot** and gets crowded. **I love it**. *Info: Turn by the Colonial and walk to the end of the street to find it.*

Jacó Bell $

For a quick taco or two or a burrito this is an amusing and quick hit.

BEST EATS IN MANUEL ANTONIO/QUEPOS

Mar y Sombra

Mar y Sombra (sun and shade) sits right at the edge of the sand, serves great seafood and steaks and really, really rocks the town starting about 10pm. This was the very first business in the area opening up to the surfers even before there was a road. Because it was built too close to the high water mark, the government attempted to bulldoze it in 2005. Loyal patrons chained themselves to the tables and a travesty was prevented. *Info: On the beach in Manuel Antonio. Tel. 2777-0510.*

Jacques Cousteau Dining Room $$$$

If you want an elegant, truly **gourmet-quality** meal in a small, quiet, **romantic setting** and you are willing to pay for it, the Jacques Cousteau Dining Room at La Mansión Inn is a good choice. Call a couple of days before you would like to dine to discuss your meal—reservations are essential. There are just a few tables.

The **wonderful wine list** is heavy on Argentinean and Chilean reds personally selected by the owner on his travels. Few realize that the restaurant will accept guests not staying at the hotel. Expect the best. *Info: In the hotel La Mansión. Tel. 2777-3489.*

Claro Que Seafood $$$

This pleasant seafood restaurant has **some of the nicest food in town**. It's a little upscale, and the honeymooners staying in the Hotel Si Como No find it to be romantic. Be sure to call for a reservation. *Info: In the Hotel Si Como No. Tel. 2777-0777.*

El Gran Escape $$$

One of the most famous places in Quepos, El Gran Escape is a nice fishermen's bar with good sandwiches and seafood grills—a very good deal. They serve North American food in a large room with lamps dangling from the ceiling and posters decorating the walls. Portions are very large. If you like palm hearts, the palm heart salad here could founder you. Pizza, huge fish sandwiches, and burgers—it's all good. I like the place a lot. Breakfast or a full meal can cost under $10. Wine is available, but large beers and larger rum and tequila drinks are popular here. No pretense: just good food. **This is the best spot in Quepos**. *Info: On the main street in Quepos. Tel. 2777-0395.*

BEST EATS IN DOMINICAL

This isn't a place for fine dining. The young crowd that frequents the area is mostly interested in filling up cheap. I ate a couple of bites of the worst pizza I have ever had in my life in Dominical. Unfortunately, that restaurant is gone so I can't whine about it anymore.

El Coco Bar & Restaurant $$$
El Coco has the same kind of local/tourist fish, burgers and faux Mexican stuff as everywhere else at similar medium to high prices. *Info: Right across the "street" from Thrusters in Dominical.*

Jungle Bistro $$$
Expect pricey creations like seared tuna crusted with black peppercorn and sesame seeds with wasabi dipping sauce and items featuring "organic" mango sauce. *Info: On the beach side in Dominical.*

Argentina Steakhouse $$$
The name says it. Expect US prices for so-so tourist steaks and chicken. *Info: On the right after you turn in to Dominical.*

Solo Bueno $$
This is an OK spot for a quick bite, sandwiches, ice cream or coffee and dessert. *Info: On the right after you turn in to Dominical.*

BEST SHOPPING
Jacó
Terra Cotta Artesanía features handmade Costa Rican art, mostly from the potteries in Guatíl. *Info: Tel. 2643-2470.*

Souvenir Nazareth is yet another souvenir store with ceramics, wooden artwork, shirts and cloths. Of course, there are also dozens of shops selling the usual fridge magnets, stickers and toucans. They are all pretty much the same. A lot of the stuff is made in Mexico or Guatemala. *Info: Tel. 2643-1678.*

Just outside Jacó, about a mile south of town on the left, is a **woodcarving shop**, where a very nice geezer named Eugenio makes wonderful furniture out of exotic woods. He doesn't have a fancy showroom or anything, but there are always lots of interesting works in progress lying about.

Manuel Antonio
Very little of interest is available in the tourist shops in Manuel Antonio. At the end of the main road near the park entrance are dozens of stalls selling the usual t-shirts, wraps, plastic toucans, beads and such.

Dominical
Shopping Center Pueblo del Rió, on the right as you drive into Dominical, is an attempt at attracting upscale tourists to stores such as Century 21, a pet shop, pharmacy, liquor store and an Internet café. It still comes across as being a little bit down-market.

BEST NIGHTLIFE
Jacó
Jacó has more happening after dark than any other beach town in Costa Rica. Entertainment options run from regular old bars to discos, Latin dance emporiums, drum-and-bass places, whorehouses, "nightclubs" and sports bars. You might like **Disco La Central**, **La Hacienda**, or the **Hollywood Nightclub**. Ladies of the night may accost you in the vicinity of the **Beatle Bar**. Use one hand to guard your wallet and the other to guard the family jewels.

Avoid anyplace with the word "nightclub" in the name because in Costa Rica this almost always means a hostess bar where girls hustle you to buy over-priced drinks in exchange for their "company."

Manuel Antonio/Quepos
There are lots of nightspots in Manuel Antonio and nearby Quepos. They generally start late, and the trendiest don't get going until after midnight. **Arco Iris** features DJs. **Monchados** has reasonably-priced Mexican and seafood and occasional live music. **Billy Beach's** is the bar at Karola's and hands out potent margaritas. **La Bodeguita**, **La Cantina**, **Epi Centro** and others rock until late. For gambling, there are **casinos** at the Hotel Kamuk in Quepos, and in the Hotel Bybloss in Manuel Antonio.

BEST SPORTS & RECREATION
BOATING, CRUISES
Jungle Crocodile Safari
If you'd like a longer look at the famous croc population of the Tárcoles River, take a boat ride with these folks. Two-hour and half-day trips in a covered launch get you right up close to the big boys (plus lots of birds). *Info: www.junglecrocodilesafari.com; Tel. 2637-0656.*

FISHING
Costa Rica's Pacific coast is one of the best places in the world for billfish, dorado and tuna. Anglers frequently raise more than 20 sails on a typical

all-day trip. Rooster fish and large snapper are also common catches. You can definitely get something for dinner. Local restaurants are familiar with anglers coming in with a huge fish they want to eat.

Los Sueños Marina near Jacó and Quepos are the main ports for big-time fishing skippers. Rates run from around $500/day to well over $2,000. Some captains will do half day trips for significantly less. You can also hire local *pangas* with outboards for about half the price of the big boats. The small *pangas* will not take you out to the billfish grounds but may be a good choice if you just want the experience of being on the water with a chance for some fish for the table.

Jacó

Based in the marina at Los Sueños, **Captain Tom's Sport Fishing** takes guests out for sailfish, dorado, tuna and marlin on his new 40-foot custom-built Luhrs with twin Yanmar 500s. He uses all Shimano tackle. He is well known to be one of the most successful captains on the coast, tagging over 1,500 sailfish every year. He uses teasers and fishes live bait with circle hooks, which makes for healthy releases.

Directly offshore from the marina are some of the best fishing grounds in Central America: **Herradura Bank** and an unnamed series of mounds further out in about 1,000 feet of water. On special request, Captain Tom will take guests 40 km south to the rarely fished **La Forruno**.

Fishing Ain't Cheap!

Big-time sport fishing is **not cheap**. Charter boats on the Pacific coast run from a low of $650 on up to over $4,500 (for one day!). Most charters can take from four to six people with comfort. You can arrange to fish in local craft called *pangas* for much less. Larger boats are usually safer and more comfortable, with life vests, radios and fish-oriented electronic goodies. Dedicated fishing lodges on the Pacific and Caribbean coasts sell **all-inclusive packages** that usually include two nights in a hotel in San José, transportation by air and boat to and from the lodge, food, lodging, all the booze you can glom, and as much time as possible fishing. **Prices run from $2,500 to $3,500 for four days fishing**. An overnight trip for much less would be possible. Call or e-mail the lodges and ask about specials. If they have an empty boat, you may be able to work something out.

One morning I went with him and we caught and released 15 sails (from 90 to 125 lbs) and a dorado, and raised a marlin, all before lunch. Book as early as you can, as he is a popular captain. *Info: www.captaintoms.com; Tel. 2637-8994, 800/515-7210 US.*

Quepos

Quepos Fishing has a variety of boats and captains available. If you can get Captain Mangara and the Frenzy, you will be doing well. Another good choice would be Ross on the Bigeye II. *Info: www.queposfishing.com; Tel. 2777-2025.*

DIVING/SNORKELING

The Central Pacific area is not particularly noted for diving, but some great dives are to be had. If you are really hard-core you can arrange for trips a little further afield from Quepos.

Manuel Antonio

Costa Rica Adventure Divers operates dive trips and PADI training. *Info: Tel. 2231-5806.*

10. THE SOUTH PACIFIC COAST

The southwestern corner of Costa Rica is **the most remote region** of the country, and features some of her most **pristine rain forests**, fantastic fishing and spectacular surfing. This sparsely populated region was historically a major gold-mining area, but the major activities today are cattle ranching and ecotourism.

HIGHLIGHTS

- **Corcovado National Park** – It's the most remote and unspoiled of Costa Rica's many parks.

- **Fishing** – The Golfo Dulce is thick with roosterfish, a resplendent and hard fighting member of the jack family. Sailfish and marlin beckon offshore.

- **Wilson Botanical Garden** – The finest botanical garden in Central America is easy to visit on your way into or out of the area.

There are no sights in this region that really make sense for a one-day visit. If you only have a day to spare, you'll have a better time on the Nicoya Peninsula or one of the rain forest areas in the north of the country around Monteverde (see previous sections).

COORDINATES

Adjacent to the border with Panama, this remote region is a long drive from San José, and most destinations are reached by long dirt roads that may be impassable in the rainy season. Airstrips at Puerto Jimenez and Golfito have regularly scheduled service, and Drake Bay and Carate are served by charter flights.

A FANTASTIC WEEKEND ON THE SOUTH PACIFIC COAST

The centerpiece of this region is the **Osa Peninsula,** the most remote and isolated area of the country. Much of the peninsula is occupied by the national park and a forest reserve. The entire area is thick with wildlife. Even outside the park's boundaries, you'll see lots of scarlet macaws and toucans. Monkeys are quite common, including the adorable little squirrel monkey (*mono tití*), which is found only here in the southern part of the country.

Thanks to several small airstrips, a weekend getaway to the Osa Peninsula is just feasible. Corcovado Adventures, which runs **Corcovado Tent Lodge Camp** (see *Best Sleeps*), offers a 3 day/2 night tour that could be the trip of a lifetime for any nature lover.

You'll take a one-hour flight from Pavas Airport to a tiny seaside landing strip at **Carate**. From here, you'll walk about 40 minutes along the beach

Best Birding

All the parks and reserves are rich in bird species. To maximize the additions to your life list, visit several parks with different types of habitat (cloud forest, dry forest, coastal mangroves, etc.) The superlative destination is remote **Corcovado**, your best bet to see something really rare. **Don't pass by Carara National Park**—it's full of tourists, but its location between northern and southern climatic regions gives it a unique mix of species, and the open landscape makes them easy to spot.

to the lodge (a member of the lodge staff will meet you at the airfield and bring your luggage along in a donkey cart). There's time for an afternoon hike in the coastal rain forest. After a hearty dinner, washed down with lots of fresh fruit juice or a couple of beers at the bar, you'll go to sleep to the sounds of the surf and the jungle.

The next day, you'll take a guided tour through the forest, including a visit to a platform high up in a tree, where you can check out the **rain forest canopy**. Much of the wildlife of the forest lives high up in the trees, invisible from the ground. A few lodges have treetop platforms like this one. It's definitely worth going up to have a look, though it may not be quite as exciting as the guides make it out to be: most of what you'll see will be little brown birds.

After a second night at the peaceful tent camp (if you can't relax here, there's no hope for you), it's time to fly back to San José. Exactly when you go depends on the tide, as the only route back to the airstrip is along the beach. *Info: 3 day/2 night tours from $370 per person, double occupancy, including lodging, meals, guides, and airport transfers. www.corcovado.com; Tel. 8386-2296, 800/673-9588 US.*

Las Cruces Biological Station/Wilson Botanical Garden

Las Cruces, located up in the mountains near the border with Panama, is one of three biological stations run by the Organization for Tropical Studies. It incorporates the world-famous **Wilson Botanical Garden**, generally considered the best in Central America, with over 1,000 species of plants. Las Cruces is about a five-hour drive from San José, but it would make an easy day trip if you're staying in the Golfito area.

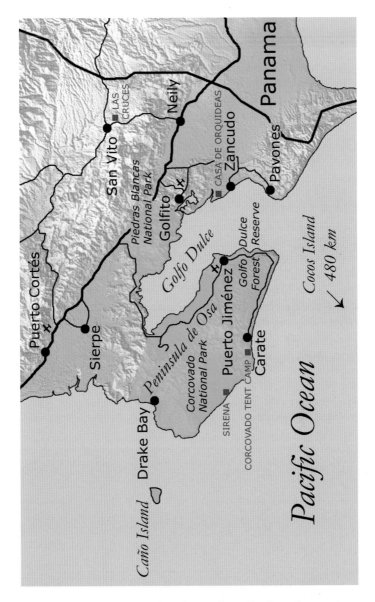

Well-maintained (but somewhat hilly) trails amble through several types of habitat. You'll experience a wealth of bromeliads, heliconias, lilies, ferns, groves of bananas, and what many call the world's largest collection of palms. The area has over 230 species of birds, including tanagers, trogons, blue-headed parrots, falcons and a profusion of hummingbirds. Monkeys and sloths are plentiful.

For really serious rain forest explorers and researchers, **Las Cruces** is a base station for exploring the nearby **La Amistad Biosphere Reserve**, the vast (472,000 hectares) and remote park that encompasses the peaks of the Talamanca mountain range.

The lodge has 12 basic but very neat and clean cabins with private bath and nice balconies, that go for about $170 double, including all meals and one guided half-day walk. *Info: Las Cruces is 5 km south of San Vito, just off the highway between San Vito and Ciudad Neily. Open year-round 8am-4pm. Half-day and full-day guided walks are available, starting at $22 for adults and $12 for kids. Night walks and dawn bird walks are also happening. Reservations are recommended. www.esintro.co.cr; Tel. 2524-0607.*

ONE TO TWO WEEKS ON THE SOUTH PACIFIC COAST

If you have a week or more, you could easily enjoy both sea and forest, either by **dividing your time between Corcovado and Crocodile Bay,** or by staying at one of the other lodges in the area, such as the **Iguana Lodge** or the remote and luxurious **Lapa Ríos** (see *Best Sleeps*), and booking a fishing trip with one of several excellent captains out of Puerto Jiménez.

Most visitors fly in, but to get the full Osa Peninsula experience, drive down from San José. This is adventure travel, and not for those with limited time. Even the drive from the main highway to Puerto Jiménez takes several hours.

The road from the highway has been improved dramatically lately but lack of maintenance and still unimproved sections make the going slow. You'll bounce along past mile after mile of cattle ranches, wondering if there can possibly be a town out here. But the road just keeps going on, until you reach grubby little Puerto Jiménez, on the coast.

Getting around by car down here requires a sturdy vehicle and plenty of time. The tiny towns are sleepy, sun-baked and seedy. The few foreigners living in them answer to a similar description. Some are globetrotting young surfers, others are colorful characters who may be hiding from the IRS or more sinister agencies (listen to *The Gringo's Tale*, a song by Steve Earle that probably wasn't written about Costa Rica, but certainly sounds as if it could have been). Most visitors to this area stay at one of the excellent jungle lodges, several of which are easily accessible by air.

Puerto Jiménez
This run-down little town is of interest to tourists only as a place to fly into and shop for supplies on the way to one of several excellent wilderness lodges in the area. It does have a couple of decent low-priced restaurants.

From here, **the road really gets interesting**, as it winds along the coast around the peninsula to Carate, the end of the road, and almost to Corcovado. You'll have to cross several rivers, some by rickety bridges, some by driving right through the water. Be sure to ask the locals about current road conditions, and don't attempt it at all during the rainy season.

In Puerto Jiménez, **Surcos Tours** offers a wide variety of local tours including rain forest treks, kayak expeditions, dolphin watching and two- to three-night guided hikes through the park. *Info: www.surcostours.com; Tel. 8603-2387.*

Changing Tide Tours offers dolphin-watching and sailing trips in the Golfo Dulce, and is highly recommended. *Info: www.changingtidetours. com; Tel. 8305-1111.*

Casa de Orquídeas
Across the bay from Puerto Jiménez, and accessible only by boat, this **charming botanical garden** has tropical wonders such as a palm tree ten feet in diameter, a lipstick tree, all sorts of exotic fruits and spices, and the usual variety of orchids, bromeliads, and their attending butterflies and

hummingbirds. Arrange a tour through your lodge, or catch a boat in Puerto Jiménez or Golfito.

Corcovado National Park

The park that is often called the "crown jewel" of Costa Rica's vast park system, and that *National Geographic* has called "the most biologically intense place on Earth," includes **the largest swath of primary forest on the Pacific coast of America**, and one of the few substantial areas of lowland tropical rain forest remaining in the world.

Corcovado is a huge park (105,000 acres) that varies in elevation from the coast to the 2,444-foot peak of Cerro Rincón. The area receives 120-240 inches of rain per year.

The area that is now the park used to be the preserve of gold miners and loggers, who caused a lot of devastation. In the 1970s the government placed restrictions on mining and logging, and established the national park, and the jungle has rapidly reclaimed the land.

This large, remote and comparatively untouristed park is arguably **the most likely place to see elusive critters** such as big cats (ocelot, margay, jaguar, puma), tapirs, river otters, peccaries and rare brocket deer, while familiar draws such as monkeys (all four species), *pizotes*, scarlet macaws,

> ### Remoter Than Thou
>
> Corcovado is often called the remotest of Costa Rica's national parks, but the prize for the most remote and unexplored park goes to **La Amistad International Park**, an enormous area of 472,000 hectares that is connected to a park across the border in Panama. Encompassing the highest peaks of the Talamanca mountain range, there are no villages or roads. The closest outposts of civilization are two research stations: **La Selva** on the northern border of the park, and **Las Cruces** near the southern edge. Either can arrange a visit, but this is no place for a day hike with the kids. Only researchers and hard-core hikers willing to camp in the backwoods will witness the wonders of this unspoiled wilderness.

toucans and orchids are plentiful. Corcovado boasts 140 species of mammals, 120 species of reptiles and amphibians, and 375 species of birds.

Corcovado is not a destination for the casual visitor. Just getting here takes some time and some planning. Some of the trails are long and rugged, with river crossings and steep climbs.

Some sections may be closed during the rainy season. The heat, the insects and all the other hazards of the rain forest are at their most intense here (except the crowds).

There are well-maintained trails around and between the various ranger stations. You can take a short hike on a fairly flat trail along the coast, or a steep one up into the interior. The really hardy can hike from the park border all the way to Sirena (16 km from Madrigal, 23 km from San Pedrillo). You'll be wading across several rivers, and **snakes are abundant**, so the rangers strongly recommend rubber boots.

The **Sirena Biological Station** is the heart of Corcovado, paradise for twitchers and wildlife lovers. If you want to see the crocodile eat the baby anteater, this is the place to come. Most tourists come to Corcovado National Park on package tours, but you're welcome to visit on your own. There are **three ranger stations** at the borders of the park: **San Pedrillo** in the northwest, **La Leona** in the southeast, and **Los Patos** in the northeast. Park headquarters is at **Sirena**, deep in the heart of the park, and accessible only by foot, plane or boat (advance reservations are required; several local

The Bug Lady

Tracie Stice (the Bug Lady), offers one of the best tours I have taken in Costa Rica. Biologist Tracie is based in Drake Bay and takes **small groups into the forest at night** with flashlights and night vision goggles to see nightlife, focusing primarily on, well, bugs. She knows more about insects than seems possible. She describes the exotic sex lives of the tiny critters, and makes it much more interesting than my high school biology teacher did. **She promises to show you thousands of spiders.** And she delivers. Her spotter walks ahead of the group looking for the unusual and fascinating, leaving Tracie time to explain and tell stories about who gets to eat whom instead of smoking a cigarette after the insect sex act. Her tour is worth a trip to Drake Bay all by itself. *Info: www.thenighttour.com; Tel. 8701-7356, 8701-7462.*

operators can arrange trips). You can camp at any of the stations. Very basic lodging and meals are available at Sirena. *Info: The entrance fee is $10 per day.*

Drake Bay

An alternate jumping-off point for Corcovado National Park is **Drake Bay**, on the northern side of the park. This is a very remote spot. There is a road connection that's supposedly passable with a 4x4 during the dry season, but most visitors arrive by plane or boat. Drake Bay is an area rather than a town. There's a small village called **Agujitas**, and a bunch of jungle lodges spread out around the large and picturesque crescent-shaped, crocodile-infested bay. A couple of operators offer dive and sightseeing trips to nearby Caño Island.

Caño Island

This small island, 20 kilometers offshore and visible from Drake Bay, is an **uninhabited biological reserve**. The forest is beautiful, but no more interesting than that of nearby Corcovado. However, an excursion to the island is a good excuse to take a boat ride and see the whales and dolphins. The island boasts some coral, and is an excellent spot for diving. Snorkeling is good when the waves are calm.

Cocos Island

The **world's largest uninhabited island** lies about 480 kilometers to the southwest of the Costa Rican mainland. The entire island is a national park. Although it has a number of birds that are found nowhere else in the world, as well as lush forest with many picturesque waterfalls, the island itself is visited almost exclusively by biological researchers. Numerous expeditions in search of pirate treasure have dug enormous holes around the island. Serious divers visit the nearby waters on liveaboard dive boats to swim with the **huge schools of scalloped hammerhead sharks**, manta rays and other large pelagic species (see *Best Sports & Recreation*).

On the eastern side of the Golfo Dulce, across the bay from the Osa Peninsula, are a couple of small villages with some lodges and fishing resorts.

Golfito

The Austrian-run **Esquinas Rain Forest Lodge,** a fine place that's popular with serious eco-adventurers, is near Golfito. Also in the area is **Banana Bay Marina**, a new full-service fishing lodge (see *Best Sleeps*). Unless you're going to one of these spots, avoid this sleazy little town at all costs.

Best Surfing

The hippest surf spot of them all is **Pavones**, where the quarter-mile-long left break comes so close to shore that you can toss a beer to passing surfers from the bar. It is extremely laid back and the endemic surfers have a reputation for being snotty and territorial. So!

Zancudo

The road to this little village is very slow going. Archipelagos of asphalt offer indications that the road was paved at one time. Huge washouts, hastily repaired in 2002, were still there and perilous in 2010.

Zancudo is local dialect for "mosquito," and these and surfers are about all you'll find here. Vultures lazily chew carcasses in the middle of the main street, a rutted dirt track. The only reason to come here is to stay at **The Zancudo Lodge** (see *Best Sleeps*), an excellent and colorful fishing lodge.

BEST SLEEPS & EATS
BEST SLEEPS IN DRAKE BAY
La Paloma Lodge $$$

Here you'll find luxury food and lodgings with an emphasis on **scuba diving**. You are right in the jungle but with a fantastic view out to sea. Rooms

are tropical, with the breeze blowing through. The lodge is high atop a hill, with incredible views out to Caño Island. Bring your binoculars to spot whales, dolphins and a host of seabirds. The rooms and open-air "ranchos" have beautiful wood décor, ceiling fans and balconies with splendid views. Prevailing westerly winds keep things reasonably cool year-round. The food is one of the most memorable things about La Paloma. Fresh fruit, local seafood and organic produce are the basis for interesting meals served in the open-air dining room/lounge. **Cheeky monkeys** will help themselves to the breakfast buffet if you don't watch out. Scrabble tournaments rage for months at a time. *Info: www.lapalomalodge.com; Tel. 2293-7502.*

Aguila de Osa $$$
Aguila de Osa is run by two wonderful tropical characters. Owners Bradd Johnson and Manager Pedro Garro are personable and interested in making sure their guests have a good time enjoy-

ing the nearby Corcovado National Park, fishing, diving or observing dolphins. The Aguila has **the best sport fishing operation in the area** and is well equipped for divers. The food is tremendous, the wine flows freely and the CD selection behind the bar is awesome. The rooms are not luxurious, but are fairly comfortable, and most have great views. Coffee is brought to your door in the morning in a thermos. You need to get it quickly, before the monkeys do. Monkeys cranked up on caffeine are not a pretty sight. **I love this place.** *Info: www.aguiladeosa.com; Tel. 2296-2190, 866/924-8452 US.*

Drake Bay Lodges

La Paloma and **Aguila de Osa** are two of several upscale lodges clustered around a small inlet. Corcovado National Park is close, so exploration activities occupy most visitors. Electricity can be unreliable. Fishing and diving are wonderful. Whales, dolphins and crocs populate the waters. Access is by a barely passable dirt road, by air or by boat.

BEST SLEEPS NEAR CORCOVADO PARK

Corcovado Adventures Tent Camp $$
Located right **at the edge of Corcovado National Park** near Carate, the tent camp is without a doubt the best and most comfortable way to enjoy **the most remote and unspoiled area** of Costa Rica. And I do mean remote—you walk on the beach for about a mile to get to the lodge (your luggage rides comfortably in a donkey cart). You can't get any further out into the jungle without actually camping.

In spite of the word "tent" in the name, it is extremely comfortable. The tents are set up over wooden platforms, and each has two beds and a nightstand inside. That's it. Bathrooms are nearby.

The food is served communally and is definitely wonderful. Shrimp, fish, steaks and local produce are well prepared and plentiful. One night when shrimp was for dinner, there were large platters with dozens and dozens of great big shrimp—more than we could eat! The piña coladas are superb.

I suppose the best thing about the lodge is that it is right next to the park. The Osa is the least disturbed area of the country and is **astoundingly rich in wildlife**. If you want to see wildlife, there are no better places to do it. Trails into the park start just outside the property. A long walk along the beach will almost certainly yield numerous animal sightings. Twitchers add significantly to their life lists from a platform set up by the lodge high in the forest canopy.

The lodge is just above the high-tide line in the palm trees above one of the most beautiful beaches I have seen anywhere. **Scarlet macaws** by the dozen hang around making a racket. Howler monkeys add to the noise. The sound of the surf never leaves you—the roar lulls you to sleep. You never want to leave. *Info: www.corcovado.com; Tel. 8386-2296, 800/673-9588 US.*

BEST SLEEPS NEAR PUERTO JIMÉNEZ
Lapa Ríos $$$$
Lapa Ríos is without doubt **the most luxurious eco-lodge in the country**. It's one of only two hotels in the country to earn a perfect sustainable tourism score of five green leaves from the Costa Rican Tourist Board. The food is superb, the rooms are unique and the location is stunning. I saw three different types of monkeys from my balcony in two days. **Toucans** chattered up a storm.

They only have 16 rooms, which are all separate luxurious bungalows. You follow a long wooden walkway through the jungle to get to your rooms.

Keep the door to the deck shut if you are not paying attention, or the **monkeys** may come in and help themselves to whatever seems interesting. The restaurant is more formal than in other nearby lodges, with separate tables and a menu with selections. Banana pancakes were brilliant.

All the usual tours and activities can be arranged, including a walk through the forest examining medicinal herbs led by a local *brujo* (witch) or medicine man, who claims to be part shaman and part showman. *Info: www. laparios.com; Tel. 2735-5130, 2735-5281.*

Iguana Lodge $$$$
This super-friendly lodge is **on the deserted Plantares Beach**, which is great for surfing, boogie boarding and long walks. Dogs are provided for beach walks if requested. The unique tropical-style rooms are luxurious, with good mattresses, fluffy pillows and excellent reading lights. Some of the showers are actually in a walled garden outside the rooms. If you like, your room can be provided with a cat.

The food is excellent (they have the best chef in Osa) and owners Toby and Lauren Cleaver keep the wine and good conversation flowing. You really have the feeling you are staying in a guest cottage at their home. **This is one of my very favorite lodges** in Costa Rica.

The location is convenient to Corcovado National Park and Puerto Jiménez. The Cleavers know all the best fishing captains and tour guides and can set you up with all the usual activities. *Info: www.iguanalodge.com; Tel. 8848-0752.*

Crocodile Bay Lodge $$$$
Crocodile Bay is **the best-run fishing lodge in the country**. Some of the older lodges ooze charm and old-style ambiance, but Crocodile Bay has set the level of competition very high. While it is still primarily a fishing lodge, there has been a great effort in recent years to appeal to the whole

family. The all-new spa is one of the nicest and most complete in Costa Rica and the lodge offers a complete series of adventure and eco tours.

Most guests are on an all-inclusive package that includes hotel and transfers to and from the airport in San José for the first and last nights in the country, flights to Puerto Jiménez, transfers to and from the local airport, room, meals, all fishing expenses and all the local beer, liquor, and house wines you can handle. If you do all of this on your own, and hire independent local captains, you will probably spend more money and have less time for fishing. Crocodile Bay is only a little more expensive than other fishing lodges in the country, and the money is not wasted.

There are 22 standard and eight deluxe rooms, as well as two 3-bedroom houses. The rooms are the nicest of any fishing lodge I have visited. Large and air-conditioned, with two queen-size beds, they have phones, AC, TV, coffee makers, safes and racks to store your fishing poles.

The food is superb, with groaning buffets of seafood, t-bone steaks, pork chops and Cajun chicken. The pool has an elaborately stocked swim-up bar where **the booze flows freely**. If you feel your daiquiri isn't strong enough, just say so and the bartender will start pouring it full of rum until you tell him to stop. There is a large, well stocked gift shop.

Fishing Director Todd Staley makes sure all fishing activities are run smoothly and efficiently. When I arrived recently for a stay, he met me just inside the door to the lobby and said, "Let's get started fishing. You can have lunch here in the lodge or there are sandwiches in the boat." We dropped our luggage in the room and were at the dock five minutes later where the motor was running ready for us. We were fishing within 15 minutes of our arrival. The sandwiches were great.

They run a fleet of 35 boats set up specifically for inshore or offshore fishing. Offshore trolling utilizes teasers with anglers waiting for interest from sails or marlin and only then tossing them a live sardine to chew on. This means you are likely to perform the whole hooking up operation yourself—much more satisfying then simply letting the mate hand you a bending rod with fish already attached, but the mates will help you as much or as little as you like.

One of the best reasons for fishing in this area is the proximity to the fishing grounds. Roosterfish are caught within a few hundred feet of the dock and the billfish are 20 miles away. The lodges out of Golfito have a little farther to run. It is not unusual to hook 10 sailfish in a day. Each night, in the bar, the results of each boat's day are posted on a white board. This practice, sadly, cuts down a bit on lying about what you caught, but what can you do? *Info: www.crocodilebay.com; Tel. 800/733-1115 US.*

BEST SLEEPS IN THE GOLFITO AREA

Esquinas Rainforest Lodge $$$

If you are serious about **eco-adventuring** and like to be out in the middle of nowhere with experienced naturalists to talk to, Esquinas may be for you. It is only a few miles  from Golfito and a mile or two off the Pan American Highway, but it's in the middle of primary and secondary rain forest, with not much else around. An Austrian group donated land for the lodge and the nearby **Gamba Biological Research Station**. The food in the restaurant is good. The pool is really amazing. A mountain stream runs right through it (cold!) and it is crystal clear and has no chemicals. There is a caiman pond on the lodge grounds but watch out! Some of the caimans are actually plastic! The rooms are basic but comfortable. If you have the oomph, you can take a long hike from the lodge over the mountain to the Golfo Dulce. *Info: Just outside Golfito. www.esquinaslodge.com; Tel. 2741-8001.*

Banana Bay Marina $$

This is a major sportfishing center, with a full-service marina and every amenity a boater could want. They have a few rooms available, all with AC and views of the marina. The Bilge Bar and Grill is probably better than it sounds. *Info: www.bananabaymarina.com; Tel. 2775-0838, 2775-1111.*

BEST SLEEPS IN ZANCUDO

The Zancudo Lodge $$$

Roy Ventura, the father of Costa Rican sport fishing, founded this world-famous fishing lodge over 25 years ago. This is **a place for serious anglers**. The rooms are air-conditioned, with all the amenities you would expect in a nice hotel anywhere, including TVs and phones.

The restaurant serves up **wonderful seafood** (snook, shrimp, tuna) and killer desserts. Roy's is right on the beach. Zancudo Beach is long and wide with world-class surfing nearby. There is almost nothing else going on in Zancudo except for a couple of pulperías and a bar or two.

The boats and equipment are top-quality and kept up-to-date. The lodge location is good for getting to the billfishing grounds. It is particularly well located for roosterfish.

I've stayed in most of the fishing lodges in Costa Rica and feel there is little real quality difference between them. When I am at other lodges, the talk always gets around to gossiping about the various lodges I've stayed at, their owners and staff. *Info: www.thezancudolodge.com; Tel. 2776-0008, 800/854-8791 US.*

BEST EATS IN PUERTO JIMÉNEZ

Head to any of the hotels and jungle lodges in this section for the best dining along the South Pacific coast. There are a couple of decent restaurants, listed below. Fair warning: **skip Juanita's Beer Garden**, often recommended to tourists. Little care is taken with the sort-of-Mexican food, and dishes are often served cold. They never had beer when I visited, and there is certainly no garden. As far as I can tell, the Chinese cook is incapable of preparing palatable Mexican food. I've given the place several chances but gave up.

Buena Esperanza $$

Also called Martina's, Buena Esperanza is a few miles outside town on the left, on the road towards Matapalo. It's really the only place to get a beer for many a mile, and serves great sandwiches and special meals. If you want a feast you will need to ask the interesting German owner, Martina, in advance. This is a great local hangout and a good stop (in fact, the only one) for a cold drink on the way to Corcovado.

Restaurante Carolina $
Right about where the bus lets out, open to the street, Carolina's is the hangout of preference for the moment, with fish and meat *casados* for $4 or less. The food is fine and cheap. Their fruit smoothies are wonderful but somehow don't last long enough.

BEST NIGHTLIFE
Puerto Jiménez
There is almost no place to party in Puerto Jiménez. Some would send you to Juanita's Beer Garden but I won't do that: they have no beer, no garden and no apologies. Instead, you need to drive outside town about six miles or so towards Matapalo and hang out at **Martina's Buena Esperanza**, the hippest spot for a hundred miles in any direction. It's just a sleepy little open-air bar on the side of the road but it rocks on the weekends. The **Pearl of the Osa**, next to Iguana Lodge, has pasta and live music on Friday nights.

BEST SPORTS & RECREATION
FISHING
Independent captain **Mike Hennessey** operates out of Puerto Jiménez, and is a real pro with his own new boat. Captain Mike is the recommended captain for many of the area lodges, so call well in advance for reservations. He can arrange for pickup. *Info: Tel. 8382-7796.*

Crocodile Bay, located near the airport in Puerto Jiménez, is the most professionally run fishing lodge in the country. The tackle and boats are newish and top quality. Big boats, little boats, spinning or trolling tackle, they have it. Most fishing is done with live bait and teasers. This guarantees a good hook-up ratio. Captains and mates speak English. The rooms are large and modern, with everything you would expect to find in a top-notch US hotel. The all-inclusive packages are a good deal, with huge

buffets, free-flowing bar, transportation in and out of San José and all the fishing you can handle. The best roosterfish action in the world starts about 500 feet from their dock. Sails, marlin, dorado and tuna choke the waters offshore. *Info: www.crocodilebay.com; Tel. 800/733-1115 US.*

The **Zancudo Lodge**, near Golfito, has a fleet of twelve 28-foot center-console boats, and operates one of the nicest lodges in the country. Over 60 IGFA world records have been set here. *Info: www.thezancudolodge.com; Tel. 2776-0008, 800/854-8791 US.*

Banana Bay Marina, also near Golfito, is home to several charter boats. Each of the captains has their own specialties, but all are quite capable of providing a world-class day of fishing. They're particularly proud of their success with **marlin**, so if you seek the man in the blue (or striped) suit, this could be the spot. *Info: www.bananabaymarina.com; Tel. 2775-0838, 2775-1111.*

You Wanna Eat It?
Most fishing operations in Costa Rica practice **catch and release**. You might keep a few filets of tuna or dorado for the table, but that prize billfish or rooster will survive to swim another day, thanks to local guides' skill at returning game fish to the water unharmed.

DIVING

Drake Bay

Most of the diving is done around a hump a mile or so off Caño Island. The visibility is not great, but there are plenty of fish. Snorkeling or diving with dolphins is always popular. Two of the lodges specialize in diving.

La Paloma has the best diving platform in the area and all the equipment you'll need. It's also a wonderful jungle lodge. *Info: www.lapalomalodge.com; Tel. 2293-7502.*

Jinetes de Osa is a comfortable lodge in Drake Bay catering to divers. *Info: www.jinetesdeosa.com; Tel. 2231-5806, 866/553-7073 US.*

Isla del Coco

The only way to get to Isla del Coco (aka **Cocos Island**), see photo below, for diving is on one of the liveaboard dive boats that take people on week

or ten-day dive trips. The dive is famous for hammerhead sharks and pelagics. Experienced divers only, please! Check out one of these **liveaboards**:

- **Undersea Hunter**. *Info: www.underseahunter.com; Tel. 2228-6613, 800/203-2120 US.*
- **Okeanos Aggressor**. *Info: www.aggressor.com; Tel. 800/348-2628 US.*

SURFING

Very hip and secret is the place known as **Punta Matapalo** on the tip of the Osa Peninsula. There are several places in Costa Rica called Matapalo but this is the one the surfers revere. The waves can get downright dangerous at times. There are no hotels or much of any place nice to stay except big-buck jungle lodges. There is only one bar or restaurant, which is **Martina's**, one of the hippest places in the whole country. People camp in the bushes or buddy up with someone renting a small house.

The very hippest surf spot of them all is **Pavones**, with its consistent quarter-mile-long left break. It's just a tiny village way out in the sticks near the Panamanian border. There is nothing going on here other than surfing, dude.

11. PRACTICAL MATTERS

AIRPORTS/ARRIVALS

Costa Rica's largest airport is **Juan Santamaría International Airport** (SJO), which is located near the San José suburb of Alajuela. Several major US airlines fly there from various hubs, including Houston, Miami and Atlanta. Costa Rica's national airline, **Avianca Costa Rica** (formerly knowed as Lacsa) offers service from several cities in the US. *Info: www. avianca.com.*

You may or may not be able to get a better deal on airfare by booking a package deal including lodging and tours through a travel agent or tour company (see below).

There are several ways to get from Juan Santamaría Airport to your destination. As you leave the terminal, just before you get outside to the sidewalk, there is a booth on the left that sells taxi vouchers for about $16. The designated taxis are right outside the door. Regular taxis are available to the right. The trip to central San José takes about a half hour, with good traffic, and costs around $20 in a regular taxi. Some of the upscale hotels have free shuttles. **Interbus** and **Grayline** operate shuttles between the airport and some of the major hotels (or, by advance reservation, to just about anywhere in the country). There's also a public bus that costs about 50 cents (the stop is on the highway directly in front of the terminal). There are several car rental agencies at and near the airport. *Info: Interbus: www.interbusonline.com; Tel. 4100-0888. Grayline: www.graylinecostarica. com; Tel. 2220-2126, 800/719-3905 US.*

Changing money at the change booths in the airport is a rip-off— you'll get 10% to 15% less than anywhere else. Pay for the taxi ride into town in US dollars at the booth, then change money at a bank in town (or use an ATM card to get some local currency).

Most flights arrive late in the day, so nearly all visitors spend a night in the area, and then get an early start the next day to fly or drive to their beach or rain forest destination. If this is your plan, you'll probably find it much more convenient to stay in one of several attractive lodgings in the area of Alajuela or Heredia, near the airport, avoiding central San José (see *Best Sleeps in San José*).

There are two internal airlines, **Nature Air** and **SANSA**. Both fly from the international airport, Juan Santamaría, and offer **daily flights to about 15 destinations around the country**. Both are pretty strict about checked baggage. SANSA charges an extra $1 per pound for anything over 30 pounds; Nature Air allows between 15 and 40 pounds per person, depending on the fare class. *Info: SANSA: www.flysansa.com; Tel. 2290-4100, 877/767-2672 US. Nature Air: www.natureair.com; Tel. 2299-6000, 800/235-9272 US.*

The international airport near **Liberia** (LIR), in the northwest of the country, is also served by several US airlines. Flying here instead of San José would be a good choice if you plan to visit the nearby Nicoya Peninsula or Rincón de la Vieja National Park. There are taxis and car rentals available at the airport, as well as a public bus to downtown Liberia. Most lodges are happy to arrange for a van from the airport, which may be the most convenient option. *Info: For information about flight schedules and facilities, see www.liberiacostaricaairport.net.*

CRUISES

Quite a few cruise ships are visiting Costa Rica these days, but most of them follow the usual cruise ship routine, stopping at only one port in the country and running quick day tours of activities close to the port. East coast cruises tend to stop at Limón, while the West coast cruises stop at Puntarenas—neither are very interesting towns, but they're convenient for wonderful day trips.

A few smaller cruise lines offer more interesting Costa Rica-oriented trips. **Lindblad Expeditions** offers a particularly nice cruise on a small 60-pas-

---

Cuban Cigars, Anyone?

Costa Ricans, and visitors, are free to enjoy wonderful Cuban cigars and rum. Many restaurants and hotels have them in stock. You can buy and smoke them guilt free—**just don't try to take them back to the US** with you. Customs agents recognize them by the paper rings.

senger ship that stops at a couple of spots on the Pacific coast of Costa Rica, and passes through the Panama Canal. Some of their cruises include stops in other parts of Panama as well. On board are scientists from the Smithsonian and other prestigious institutions who lead hikes and give talks on tropical biology, birds and wildlife, conservation and other topics of interest to more discerning travelers.

Cruise lines that offer stops in Costa Rica include:
- **Celebrity Cruises**, *www.celebritycruises.com.*
- **Cunard**, *www.cunard.com; Tel. 800/7cunard.*
- **Holland America**, *www.hollandamerica.com; Tel. 877/932-4259.*
- **Lindblad Expeditions**, *www.expeditions.com; Tel. 800/EXPEDITION.*
- **Star Clippers**, *www.starclipperscruises.com; Tel. 877-828-4774.*
- **Princess Cruises**, *www.princess.com; Tel. 800/PRINCESS.*
- **Seabourn Cruise Line**, *www.seabourn.com; Tel. 800/929-9391.*
- **Windstar Cruises**, *www.windstarcruises.com; Tel. 800/258-7245.*

PACKAGE TOURS

Lots of companies offer package tours, whether it's an all-inclusive deal including airfare from the States, or a shorter tour for only part of your trip within Costa Rica. Even if you're the independent type, you may want to consider a package tour, at least for part of your trip. By coordinating charter flights and ground transportation, a tour company can get you to remote areas fairly quickly, eliminating much of the hassle. Here are some of the best of the large tour companies.

Costa Rica Expeditions is perhaps the largest and best-known operator in the country. They manage a couple of lodges, located in the most popular wildlife areas in the country: Monteverde and Tortuguero They can arrange anything there is to do in Costa Rica, from a morning trip to a coffee plantation to a weeklong trek through the wilderness. Costa Rica Expeditions is best known as the original organizer of rafting trips in Costa Rica. Some of their most popular tours are their **"multi-sport" tours** involving rafting, surfing, hiking and a variety of other sporty activities. One of the things they do best is put together small groups of like-minded travelers of similar ages for hikes through Corcovado National Park. *Info: www.costaricaexpeditions.com; Tel. 2257-0766, 2521-6099.*

Insight Costa Rica is a small Alajuela-based company that arranges a variety of package tours. They also rent vans with drivers on a daily or weekly basis, which is an extremely convenient way to get to remote areas. *Info: www.insightcostarica.com; Tel. 2430-2929.*

Costa Rica Outdoors specializes in helping visitors set up customized itineraries based on their individual interests and budgets. If you are a hard-core angler, they can arrange for you to spend several days dragging in tarpon on the Caribbean coast followed by several days tugging on sailfish in the Pacific. They have a very handy form on their website that lets you enter your interests, budget, etc. and receive back a handcrafted suggested itinerary including hotels, tours and transportation. Kids, seniors, active hikers or beach and hammock wallowers can all be accommodated. They have been around since 1994, and publish a magazine, also called Costa Rica Outdoors. *Info: www.costaricaoutdoors.com; Tel. 2231-0306, 2231-0673 or 800/308-3394 US.*

Probably the number two tour company in Costa Rica, **Horizontes** offers group and individual travel plans. Their approach is to send their tours to the hotels and local tour operators they have experience with throughout the country. *Info: www.horizontes.com; Tel. 2222-2022.*

One of the larger agencies in Costa Rica, San José-based **Swiss Travel Service** specializes in incentive and group travel. *Info: www.swisstravelcr. com; Tel. 2282-4898.*

ACTUAR is a community-based rural tourism specialist. *Info: www.actu-arcostarica.com; Tel. 2290-7514, 866/393-5889 US.*

Guided tours of all kinds are big, big business in Costa Rica. Wildlife observation tours are the big banana, but all kinds of sports and activities are on offer as well. Horseback riding, mountain biking, kayaking, canoeing, whitewater rafting, caving, climbing and rappelling, underwater basket weaving—you name it, you can do it on a guided tour.

I highly recommend using a local guide when you visit the rain forest. You'll see and learn much more than you would on your own. The best forest experiences happen in small groups. The fewer people on your jungle hike, the better—you'll be quieter and therefore see more wildlife, and the guide can spend more time answering your questions and addressing your particular areas of interest.

There are four ways to go about arranging tours:

1) You can **book a package** that includes flights, hotels, meals and guides, over the web or with a local or Costa Rican travel agency before you even leave home. If you want to visit one of the more remote regions, and have limited time, this is your best option, though it probably won't be the cheapest.

2) Each of the major national parks has a pool of **licensed guides**, who take a three-year college course to become naturalist tour guides. You can sometimes just show up at the ranger station and arrange for a guide, but at the more popular parks, you'll be wiser to call ahead and make a reservation. At the more popular parks, unlicensed guides hang around at the entrance drumming up custom, so be careful.

3) Every hotel in the country is familiar with the **local tours** that are on offer, and will be happy to help you make arrangements. They may tack on an extra fee.

4) In the more touristed areas, **freelance tour operators** hang around the beach or the main street and offer their services. You must use your judgment as to whether they can be trusted.

GETTING AROUND
By Air
In remote areas, roads may be in poor repair or non-existent, so travel by small plane is a popular option. If you want to see a lot in a short time, it's the best way to travel. Two domestic airlines, **SANSA** (*www.flysansa. com; Tel. 2290-4100, 877/767-2672 US*) and **Nature Air** (*www.natureair. com; Tel. 2299-6000, 800/235-9272 US*) offer flights to a couple dozen destinations around the country. Reasonably priced charter companies can fly you to even the most remote jungle lodges. If you have more than four people in your group, it may be a better deal to arrange for a charter. Charters are usually more convenient, leaving and arriving at a time to suit you. Some small airports are served only by charter.

Both domestic airlines serve most of the same destinations within Costa Rica. Nature Air also flies to Bocas del Toro in Panama and Managua in Nicaragua. SANSA is part of a larger business group (Grupo Taca) and can arrange for connections to Panama, Nicaragua, Honduras, Cuba and Guatemala.

Other than the San José and Liberia airports described above, the rest are little more than landing strips with few or no facilities. Some of the smallest are nothing but a reasonably level field of grass. Little boys with sticks drive the cows off just before each landing.

Car Rental

Renting your own car offers the maximum in flexibility, but the poor state of the roads puts some people off. Anything that doesn't have 4-wheel drive is likely to be inadequate once you get off the major highways (and if you don't plan to drive off the major highways, there's little reason to rent a car). Fortunately, most rental agencies have a good selection of 4WD vehicles, from cute little Subarus to hulking SUVs. You'll save a lot of hassle, and possibly some money as well, if you reserve a rental car online before leaving home.

I've had good experiences with **Europcar**. *Info: www.europcar.com; Tel. 2257-1158*. The oddly-named **Toyota** is another good local company. *Info: www.toyotarent.com; Tel. 2258-5797*. You can rent an older, cheaper car from **4x4 Rent a Car**. *Info: www.4x4rentacar.com; Tel. 4034-7731*.

Rental cars are not cheap in Costa Rica. The government has a monopoly on insurance, and all car rentals include the cost of mandatory insurance. Even if you already have your own insurance through your regular insurance company or through your credit card, you'll have to pay for the government insurance.

Gasoline usually costs about the same as it does in the US. Filling stations (*bombas* or *gasolineras*) are rare outside of towns, so it's prudent to top up whenever you see one. The government runs all the gas stations, so the prices are generally the same all over the country. There is no need to shop around for the best price.

Police with radar are common and are quite willing to hand out speeding tickets. Be very careful approaching villages if you are cruising fast on the highway. Speed limits are almost always much lower in towns and the cops (*las pacas*), often spend all day hanging around by the side of the highway with their radar guns.

Taxis

Taxis are reasonably priced and convenient. Within towns, they're the best way to get around. After dark in San José and other cities, they're the only safe way to get around. In San José, drivers are theoretically required to charge by the meter (called a *maría*), but elsewhere fares are usually negotiable. A word to the wise: any time you take a taxi in the developing world, be sure to agree on a fare before riding anywhere.

A taxi can also be an affordable way to get to rural destinations, or just to take a tour around the countryside, especially if you're with a group.

Probably the best way to enjoy your trip around Costa Rica is to **hire a driver and their vehicle**. If you have more than four or so people in your party it becomes an economically viable alternative.

For example, **Esterling Alfaro** has his own 12-passenger air-conditioned van, and is available for one- or multi-day trips around the country. He knows all the little out-of-the-way places to stop for a good bite to eat and explains, tells stories and educates as much or as little as you like. For visitors planning trips with specific interests such as birding, visiting national parks, or rural tourism, he will be happy to put together suggestions and quote a price. *Info: www.insightcostarica.com; Tel. 2430-2929.*

Buses

Interbus and **Grayline** have frequent scheduled service between most Costa Rican tourist destinations, using small to medium-sized tourist buses. Prices are usually excellent, and they will often pick you up at your hotel. *Info: Interbus: www.interbusonline.com; Tel. 4100-0888. Grayline: www.graylinecostarica.com; Tel. 2220-2126, 800/719-3905 US.*

The public bus system covers most of the country, is reasonably punctual, and is very cheap. Some popular tourist areas are served by faster (and pricier) air-conditioned express buses in addition to the usual Central American torture buses (some of which are old US school buses).

BANKING & CHANGING MONEY

Costa Rica's monetary unit is the *Colón* (plural *Colones*). At press time, the interbank exchange rate was just under 540 to the US Dollar (one US Dollar = 540 Colones). *Info: See www.oanda.com for current rates.*

Many travelers don't really understand how currency exchange works, and this ignorance can cost you money. Here's the straight scoop. Every time you change currencies, you pay a fee in the form of the spread between the buy and sell exchange rates. The interbank rate, the rate at which banks exchange money among themselves, lies midway between the buy and sell rates, so the bank earns a fee on every transaction. Some currency-exchange places also charge a small fixed commission, the purpose of which is to prevent you from comparing rates between different exchange outlets. Even if a place trumpets "No Commission!" you're still paying a fee. To see if you're getting a good deal or a bad deal, look at the spread.

Credit cards and ATM cards offer the best spreads (about 2% from the interbank rate for credit cards, 3-4% for ATMs), and using them in Costa Rica has gotten much easier in recent years. ATMs are fairly common, and nowadays most medium-sized towns have an ATM that will accept US cards belonging to one of the major ATM networks (Honor, Cirrus, etc). In the past, most Costa Rican ATMs accepted local bank cards only. Unfortunately, many US banks add exorbitant fees for international ATM use, so check with your bank before your trip.

Most substantial tourist-oriented businesses will accept credit cards (Visa is far more widely accepted than MasterCard or American Express). Smaller places may not accept cards, and some places will tack on an extra fee for using plastic (technically, this is against the credit card companies' rules, but places do it anyway). Sadly, many US credit cards have recently begun charging ridiculous fees to use your card internationally. Also note that, as a precaution against fraud, many issuers will refuse any international charges until you call them (there's usually a toll-free number on the back of the card) and confirm that it's really you using the card. Be sure to contact your card company before your trip and ask what the deal is.

Changing money at banks is a bureaucratic nightmare, but they may offer the best exchange rates for cash. Most hotels will gladly change money for you, but will probably offer an unfavorable rate. Changing money at the change booths in the airport is a big rip-off (see above). As for the touts offering to change money on the street, don't even talk to them.

Most banks will accept only US Dollars (UK Pounds or Euros maybe, but anything else, forget it). Travelers' checks are not widely accepted, and are subject to extra fees.

Most businesses will accept US Dollars (and give your change in *Colones*), but you will get a worse price than you would if you paid in local currency. While large hotels and tour operators follow the daily exchange rates, smaller businesses tend to use a rough-and-ready-rate, such as 540 *Colones* to the Dollar. Depending on the current interbank rate, this may be a decent deal or a bad deal.

Costa Rican *Colones* are not convertible outside the country, so remember to change any leftover cash back to Dollars before leaving, or squander it in the duty-free shop at the airport. The exchange desk at the airport will exchange no more than $50 worth at a time.

BUSINESS HOURS
Most businesses are open from around 9am to 5 or 6pm Monday through Friday, and perhaps Saturday morning. Hours tend to be longer in larger cities and tourist areas. Many businesses and offices close for two hours at lunchtime. Banks in small towns may have very limited hours. Most non-tourist-oriented businesses are closed on Sunday.

CLIMATE & WEATHER
Costa Rica has an amazing variety of climates for such a small country. Generally speaking, the Pacific north is hot and dry during the winter months, a little like California, but is rainy and humid the rest of the year. The south and the Caribbean coastal region have more typical tropical weather: hot, humid and rainy.

The Central Valley has consistently pleasant temperatures, always between 49 and 92 degrees Fahrenheit. High in the mountains, such as around Chirripó, it can actually get quite cold, even below freezing on occasion.

There are two main seasons. The **dry season** lasts from November through April, and is the main tourist season. The **"green season"** (which sounds more appealing than "rainy season") lasts from May through October, and sees far fewer tourists. Most areas of the country do get a lot of rain during this season, and some remote regions, especially in the south, can become almost inaccessible by road. However, other areas, such as the northern Pacific region, see far less rain. Prices can be much lower during the green season, and the crowds are gone.

CONSULATES & EMBASSIES
The **US embassy** is located in Pavas. *Info: http://costarica.usembassy.gov; Tel. 2519-2000.*

The **Canadian embassy** is in central San José. *Info: www.canadainternational.gc.ca/costa_rica; Tel. 2242-4400.*

The **UK embassy** is also in central San José. *Info: https://www.gov.uk/government/world/costa-rica; Tel. 2258-2025.*

ELECTRICITY

Costa Rica uses **110-volt AC, the same as in the US**, and the plugs are the same. Grounded (3-prong) plugs are not common, and the general level of **electrical safety is low**. Cheaper lodgings may feature "suicide showers," little electric heaters attached to the showerhead, sometimes with poorly insulated connectors (we've heard no reports of anyone actually being killed by one of these contraptions, which are also known as "widow makers," but *do not touch them*). Remote lodges get their power from generators, which may be turned off at night, and may deliver dodgy voltage.

EMERGENCIES & SAFETY

Crime

Compared to other Central American countries, Costa Rica is pretty safe, but thievery of various kinds does happen, and violent crime against tourists is not unheard-of. Follow a few precautions, and you should have no problems:

- As everyone will tell you, it isn't safe to walk around the streets of San José or other cities at night. Using the public bus system after dark may be dodgy as well. **At night, always take a taxi**.
- Never, ever leave any valuables in parked cars. In fact, in San José it's probably unwise to park anywhere other than a watched hotel parking lot.
- Be on the alert for **pickpockets** in any crowded situation, especially at airports, bus stations and such places. Not only cities, but also highly touristed parks such as Monteverde and Carara have their share of thieves.
- In some parks, **walking alone on isolated trails is not recommended**. Always check in at the ranger station, and hike in groups, preferably with a local guide.
- Walking on beaches at night is generally not a good idea.

I highly recommend a money belt. Not the external "fanny pack," but a small flat belt that goes around your waist (there are similar things that go around your neck) *under your clothes*. With your passport, plane ticket and main cash stash zipped up out of sight, you can relax and enjoy your trip (of course, you keep a small roll of walking-around money in a pocket, so you never have to pull out your money belt in public). Money belts are available at any good luggage shop or (much cheaper) at discount stores. As for those fanny packs, they're famous around the world as magnets for thieves and con artists.

Be on your guard whenever you hand over cash for tours and other local services. Make sure you're dealing with a legitimate employee, and get a receipt. When paying by credit card, keep a close eye on your card, and make sure any unused charge slips (for example, for a rental car deposit) are destroyed.

Petty theft is not the only type of crime to watch out for. **Con men** run various investment scams on tourists and retirees. If you're doing any kind of business, buying real estate or investing in the country, be extra careful to deal only with reputable firms, and, most definitely, seek advice from a local third party such as a lawyer or accountant before signing anything or parting with any dough.

Recently, several high-profile scams have been exposed, involving extremely high returns on cash investments. 30% return per month for investments of at least $100,000 is a typical offering. Of course, the monthly payments stop well before you've earned your original investment back. Be careful about pitches for depositing money in back street "banks." If it sounds too good to be true, it is.

In many Latin American countries the police are famous for demanding informal "fines," to be paid in cash on the spot, for real or imagined traffic violations. This behavior is rare in Costa Rica, but we have heard reports that it does occur. If you do get cited, don't give the cops any cash, but make sure they give you a paper traffic ticket, which you will have to pay at a bank.

Unlike some tropical vacation destinations, **Costa Rica is not particularly tolerant of marijuana or drugs**. Laws are just as strict as those in the US, or even more so. You may be offered *mota* or *ganja*, especially on the Rasta-flavored Caribbean coast, but buying on the street exposes you to many dangers, including being ripped off or turned over to the authorities.

If you travel with prescription drugs, be sure they are clearly labeled and, if possible, in the original containers (it's currently illegal to import prescription drugs into the US).

Police can ask for ID at any time, so keep yours with you. On the roads, you may occasionally pass through a police checkpoint. Have your passport and the car's papers available.

Prostitution is legal in Costa Rica (as in most places outside the US), and "sex tourism" is big business. The meat market at the Blue Marlin Bar at the Hotel del Rey in San José is world-famous. Abuse of minors is a sore point with the authorities, who do not want Costa Rica to gain a reputation as "another Thailand." Having sex with anyone under 18 is strictly illegal.

HEALTH
Costa Rica's health care system is decent. In fact, "health tourists" come here to get medical treatment at bargain rates, especially plastic surgery. There's a network of public hospitals throughout the country.

In an emergency, dial 911, or 128 for an ambulance.

For non-emergency health needs, you'll probably get better and quicker service from a private doctor or clinic, which you can find in the phone book (the Spanish for "doctor" is *médico*).

The health hazards here are the same ones you'll encounter when pursuing touristy activities in any tropical country. Be very careful about exposure to the sun: it can hurt you even on cloudy days. **Pack plenty of insect repellent**, with DEET (forget about milder remedies such as Skin-So-Soft—the mosquitoes down here will just laugh at that stuff).

Food and water are generally safe. Montezuma is less vengeful here than in some other tropical destinations. To be on the safe side, drink bottled water and use it to rinse any fruits that you don't peel or cook. No shots are required for travel to Costa Rica. Malaria and other tropical diseases are rare.

Poisonous snakes are common throughout the country, but **snakebites are rare**. When hiking in the forest, watch your step at all times, and don't stick your hand in anywhere it doesn't belong. A stout pair of **hiking boots** is a very good idea for several reasons. Slipping in the mud and spraining your ankle is more likely than getting bit by a *terciópelo*, and it could ruin your holiday.

Travelers with special health concerns should note that remote jungle lodges have limited ability to evacuate you in a medical emergency: if something happens to you, it could be hours or days before you get to a hospital.

ETIQUETTE
Ticos are great ones for **politeness**—when they meet, there's a great deal of handshaking, "how's the family?" and so forth, before any business gets discussed. Greet your new friends in the morning with *¿Cómo amaneció?* which literally means "How did you wake up?" The word *buenas* serves as an all-purpose greeting, short for the more formal *buenas mañanas/tardes/noches* (good night/afternoon/evening). See the *Essential Spanish* section at the end of this chapter for more pleasantries.

Ticos tend to be a *little* more punctual than some other Latin Americans, but don't get too upset when people show up fashionably late. The phrase *hora americana* means that something is supposed to happen more or less on time, whereas *hora tica* means the usual dithering around.

Even though you're in the tropics, please don't dress as if the whole country is a beach. At all-inclusive resorts and funky little tourist towns, beach bum attire is fine, but in places like banks, stores, etc. you'll notice that the locals wear long pants, shirts, and even jackets and ties, just as we do at home (some older guys wear the traditional *guayabera* shirt in lieu of a tie). Walking around in shorts and flip-flops marks you instantly as a tourist. Ticos almost always dress better then their North American visitors.

Tico? Gringo?
Costa Ricans call themselves *ticos* (or *ticas* if they are female). The term comes from the Costa Rican habit of adding the *-ico* or *-ica* diminutive ending to words. It is not in the least impolite for them to refer to us as *gringos/gringas*. The word *estadounidense* means someone from the US. *Norteamericano* has a similar meaning, encompassing Canadians as well.

If you see someone in ragged shorts or bathing suit and a t-shirt—it's a tourist. Flip-flops are okay in most places, but you may want to wear shoes in nice restaurants.

You might notice that Ticos rarely point at things with their fingers as we do in the US. Watch carefully and you'll see them pursing their lips and "pointing" with their lips and a head movement. Try it yourself: just make a kissy face (but don't actually make the kissy noise) and kind of bob your chin in the direction you wish to indicate. The locals won't think it's odd at all, but you might want to shed the habit before you go back to the office after your vacation.

LAND & PEOPLE

Costa Rica is located in Central America, on a narrow isthmus between the Caribbean Sea and the Pacific Ocean (only 75 miles from sea to sea at the narrowest point). Her neighbors are Nicaragua to the north and Panama to the south.

The backbone of the country is formed by several rugged mountain ranges, part of the range that runs all along the Pacific coast of America, from the Rockies to the Andes. In the north are the Guanacaste, Tilarán, and Central ranges, some of them active volcanoes, while to the south the Talamanca range includes the country's highest peak, **Cerro Chirripó** (12,530 feet).

Costa Rica has a huge variety of landscapes for such a small country (just 20,000 square miles or 51,100 square kilometers, about the same size as West Virginia), which has led several writers to describe it as a tiny continent in and of itself. Sand beaches and mangrove swamps, open savannah and impenetrable rain forest, coastal jungle, high cloud forest and even paramo, or "wet desert"—each forms its own unique ecosystem of animals and plants adapted to local conditions.

The **Central Valley** (*Valle Central*) is located on a high plateau with fertile soil and a pleasant temperate climate. It was here that the first major Spanish settlements were founded, and it's here that almost two thirds of the population lives today. Here is the capital, San José, and the smaller cities of Cartago, Alajuela and Heredia, with almost all the country's industry and most of the coffee plantations. It's a pleasant area of well-ordered farms and woodlands.

The **Pacific coast** is very rough, dotted with bays and little islands. The hilly **Nicoya Peninsula** in the north was for many years a sparsely-populated region of small villages, but today it is home to dozens of new real estate developments, as well as some of Costa Rica's most upscale resorts, with more on the way.

The steep coast south of Nicoya is the closest coastal area to the Central Valley, so it's no surprise that Costa Rica's biggest resort towns are here: Jacó, Quepos and Manuel Antonio. South along the coast sprawl vast palm-oil plantations with little company towns where the workers live.

In the southwest corner of the country is the **Osa Peninsula**, a remote and sparsely inhabited region that was once the haunt of loggers and gold miners. Today much of the region is a nature preserve, the largest remaining area of primary forest on the Pacific coast of America.

The **Caribbean coast** is far smoother than the Pacific, with an almost continuous swath of wild and deserted beaches from Nicaragua to Panama. The northern coast is very low, with a labyrinth of canals, marshes, wetlands and rain forest stretching for miles inland from the coast. Halfway down the coast is the country's second-largest city, the grubby port town of Limón.

Agriculture is an important and highly visible part of the economy, especially coffee in the Central Valley and bananas on both coasts, as well as pineapples, sugar, rice and beans (of course), and beef. However, Costa Rica is by no means a banana republic. On the contrary, the economic breakdown reads more like that of a typical "first-world" country: 6% agriculture, 22% industry and 72% services.

Small industries include microprocessors, food processing and textiles. Tourism is an ever-growing part of the economy, recently joined by modern services such as offshore banking and internet gambling.

Most of Costa Rica's 4.7 million people are poor by North American standards, but the country is one of Latin America's greatest success stories, with a per capita Gross Domestic Product (GDP) of $13,000 and a poverty rate of only 16%. The government provides a respectable roster of social services, including state-funded medical insurance and a social security plan. Levels of literacy and education are high. The level of environmental consciousness is also high. Costa Rica's system of national parks and protected areas is a model for the world. Most of the country's electricity comes from renewable hydropower, and the government has announced an ambitious goal of making Costa Rica "carbon neutral" by 2021.

The Ticos have **strong traditions of independence and egalitarianism**, which arise from the colonial past. The typical Latin American colony was a rigidly stratified society, with slaves at the bottom and wealthy plantation owners at the top. Not so in Costa Rica, where most people were of fairly pure Spanish blood, and all were poor but proud subsistence farmers who had to work together for the good of all. At least, that's the idealized version of history that informs the Tico self-image.

Unlike other countries in Central and South America, indigenous people make up only a small percentage of the population. 94% of Costa Ricans are *mestizos*, of mostly Spanish descent.

Only a few Blacks were brought to Costa Rica back in the slave days. Most of the Black folks in the country (3% of the population) are descendents of Jamaicans who came in the 19th century to work on the banana plantations. In the bad old days, they were prohibited from spending the night in the Central Valley, which tended to concentrate their numbers on the southern Caribbean coast. Although the constitution of 1949 abolished legal discrimination, most of the Blacks (or Creoles) continue to live in the region today.

Native Americans now make up only about one percent of Costa Rica's population. However, there are a few groups who still live somewhat as they did in pre-Colombian times in remote forest regions.

On the Nicoya peninsula, you can still find traces of the traditional culture of the **Chorotegas**, especially in the village of Guaitíl, famous for its traditional pottery. The **Borucas** live in remote settlements near the southern Pacific coast.

The most isolated indigenous tribes are the **Cabécar** and the **Bribri** Indians, who live a traditional lifestyle way up in the jungles north of the Talamanca mountain range.

Roman Catholics account for 76 percent of Costa Ricans. As elsewhere in Latin America, Catholicism is a major part of the culture. The Creoles of the Caribbean coast are traditionally Protestants, and a number of Evangelical denominations thrive throughout the country. Several groups belonging to traditional Christian sects have settled in the country, seeking a remote place far from the sinful US. The best known are the Quakers, who founded the town of Monteverde in the 1950s.

INTERNET ACCESS

Costa Rica is getting wired up rapidly. E-mail is a good alternative to the unreliable postal service. **RACSA** (*www.racsa.co.cr*) is the largest internet provider, offering both dial-up and broadband (cable) service. Internet cafés are common throughout the country. Many larger hotels offer internet service (with the exception of the more remote wilderness lodges, which may be out of reach of the telephone network). Some post offices also offer internet access for a fee. Wireless access in hotels is not uncommon.

You can find local internet cafés on some of the internet directory sites. See the list of Costa Rica-oriented internet directories and search engines at the end of this chapter.

LANGUAGE

The language of Costa Rica is **Spanish**, in its Latin American variant, which differs slightly from the Castilian Spanish spoken in Spain. It's not difficult to travel in Costa Rica without knowing a word of Spanish, as English is widely spoken in all tourist areas (in fact, you'll find that the owners of wilderness lodges and other tourist-oriented businesses are often from the US or Europe).

However, any experienced traveler will tell you that knowing a few key words will greatly enhance your trip. *Por favor* (please) and *gracias* (thank you) are the most useful, and using them liberally will smooth your way to a remarkable extent. And of course, you're sure to quickly learn the all-purpose Costa Rican expression: *pura vida*.

If you do want to learn Spanish, Costa Rica is an excellent place to do so. Hundreds of **language schools** cater for beginners and experts, dabbling vacationers or long-term residents. Some offer accommodations in wonderful rain forest or beachside locations.

The **National Registration Center for Study Abroad** is an organization that will help you choose and register for any of dozens of language schools around the world. They evaluate language schools, select the ones that they consider the best, and offer pre-registration to the schools on their approved list, which includes five schools in Costa Rica. *Info: www. nrcsa.com.*

Other language schools include **Intensa** (*www.intensa.com*), which has four locations in San José; **CPI** (*www.cpi-edu.com*), with campuses in Heredia, Monteverde and Playa Flamingo; and **Escuela d'Amore** (*www. escueladamore.com*) near Manuel Antonio.

Some of the residents of the southern Caribbean coast speak a local dialect of English, similar to the Patois spoken in Jamaica. Several Native American languages such as Bribri and Cabécar are spoken at various places throughout the country.

LODGING
Costa Rica has a full range of different types of lodgings. You can stay in a hermetically sealed concrete-and-glass tower, or in a jungle *cabina* with no solid walls—just a floor, roof, screens and you and the toucans. You can luxuriate at an all-inclusive beachfront resort with a championship golf course and an elaborate pool, or be an ecotourist at a remote tropical ecology research station where scientists show visitors how they study the mating habits of howler monkeys.

I have selected the best hotels and lodges of several types, rustic to modern, moderate to stratospherically expensive, and I describe them here for you to make your selection, according to the type of travel that interests you.

All of the hotels listed here are more or less up to North American standards, with a few notable exceptions. Some are luxurious by international standards, and some are interesting for other reasons.

Expect some of the more remote lodges to lack air conditioning, electricity or hot water. The only way to make a phone call may be via a super-expensive satellite link.

Insects are a part of everyday life in the tropics in even the most hygienic establishments. I'm never surprised to find a stray bug or two in even the snobbiest places in the country. Bugs happen.

Lodging Prices	
$	Basic: $75 or less
$$	Budget: $75-125
$$$	Midrange: $125-200
$$$$	First-class: $200-300
$$$$$	Luxury: $300 and up

Remember that you don't necessarily need to worry about how to get to your lodge. Some of the remote ones are very complicated to find on your own, but a piece of cake if you let them make travel arrangements for you. Most are happy to arrange transport from the airport to their door, as well as lining up guides for local tours and activities.

Prices shown are for two people in one room during high season. There's a 16% tourist tax, which may or may not be included in quoted rates. Rooms have private bath unless otherwise noted. Note that some lodges offer only package prices, which include lodging, food, and perhaps transportation and tours, so it may be hard to compare prices.

NEWSPAPERS

Several newspapers in Spanish and at least one in English serve Costa Rica. Tourism-oriented newspapers come and go, but the *Tico Times* is a solid and well-written English-language weekly. Visiting their web site (*www.ticotimes.net*) is an excellent way to get in the mood before your trip. Their weekly fishing report is a must-view for all anglers aiming at Costa Rica. *La Nación* (*www.nacion.com*) is a conservative daily paper. *La Prensa Libre* (*www.prensalibre.cr*) and *La Republica* (*www.larepublica.net*) are other, perhaps less conservative dailies.

PASSPORT REGULATIONS

Passports are required for entry. Citizens of the US, Canada, the UK, Australia and New Zealand (as well as most European countries) are permitted to stay in Costa Rica for up to 90 days without a visa. Officially, your passport must be valid for more than six months from the date of entry, or you will be refused admission. *Info: For the complete list of visa requirements for different countries, see www.visitcostarica.com/ict/paginas/informacionturistica.asp.*

If you want to stay for more than 90 days, the best thing to do is simply leave the country overnight and come back for another 90 days. It is possible to get an extension (*prórroga de turismo*) from the immigration office ( ), but the bureaucratic nightmares involved make this option impractical.

There's a **departure tax of $29 per person**, which you must pay at the airport before checking in. You have to show a receipt for the tax before you can check in, so be sure you get this done as soon as you arrive in the airport. Some hotels can collect the tax and give you a receipt ahead of time, although they may tack on a fee. You can pay with a credit card, but this may also subject you to an additional fee.

POSTAL SERVICES

Costa Rica's postal service (*correos*) is notoriously slow and inefficient. You can expect mail from Costa Rica to the States or Europe to take at least two weeks, if it arrives at all. Fortunately, most hotels and tour operators in Costa Rica are used to doing business by e-mail. For important packages, use FedEx or DHL, both of which have offices in San José. San José's main post office is at Avenida 1, Calle 2. There's also a small postal museum. *Info: www.correos.go.cr.*

RESTAURANTS

Restaurants in Costa Rica vary from local **open-air eateries** roasting chickens over an open fire (delicious!) to attempts at **world-class fine dining** with linen napkins and sorbet between courses (delicious!) and of course, everything in between. As a tourist or a short-term visitor you are offered a small but interesting range of eateries somewhere between these two extremes. Be sure to break out of the tourist herd a couple of times for a local *casado* plate lunch, and stop in at one of the top tables in the country for a night of fine dining.

Expect to pay about the same prices you would pay in the US for restaurant meals. Expect meat, fish, pasta and vegetable meals like those served in the US, but think fresh. They don't use a lot of frozen stuff in Costa Rica, yet. The wonderful fresh seafood and flavorful tropical fruits are enough by themselves to satisfy any foodie. The **delicious Costa Rican coffee** alone is worth a trip!

Be aware that good hotels often have good restaurants. In many areas of the country, hotels and lodges are where you will find the fancy eats. Most lodges, even remote jungle lodges, are interested in having you come for dinner even if you are not a guest. Call first.

Typical Costa Rican cuisine (known as *comida típica*) is easy to find at local restaurants throughout the country, especially at the small cafés called *sodas*. Such restaurants are usually reasonably cheap, and can be quite good. A typical plate is called a *casado* (literally, "married"), and consists of a big piece of meat or fish, one or more vegetables (often a fried plantain and/or a pile of chopped cabbage), and a large helping of rice and beans. Many travelers give *comida típica* a bad rap, because the beans and rice (*gallo pinto*), served at all meals, can get boring, and because cooks tend to go heavy on the lard and the salt.

Fresh fish and seafood are excellent, but sadly not as readily available as you might like. Although seafood is found aplenty in Costa Rican waters, it tends to be expensive locally, as most of what is caught is exported. By no means all the seafood served is fresh. You know you're getting really fresh fish at a fishing lodge, or at a funky local beach shack where you see the cook buying from a local fisherman. At that touristy restaurant in San José or Monteverde, however, you are likely to be presented with an unspectacular frozen fish or shrimp.

San José and, to a lesser extent, other cities, feature a range of restaurants including French, Italian, Chinese, Mexican and other worldwide favorites. Eateries in tourist areas serve American favorites such as burgers and pizza. The results can be very good, or they can be lame and overpriced.

In most of the country, your dining choices will be between hearty-but-monotonous *comida típica* and sometimes imperfectly executed international cuisine. In some of the finer resorts and wilderness lodges however, the style of cookery is so different from either of these options, and yet so uniquely Costa Rican, that I have elevated it to a separate category, which, for want of a better term, we shall call **resort cuisine** (or how about neo-Tico?).

Resort cuisine is based on fresh local ingredients, but influenced by the modern North American and European cooking tradition, with its emphasis on low-fat cooking and healthy ingredients, and by a cosmopolitan mix of the world's cuisines, particularly Eastern ones. This happy culinary marriage is the result of two trends. Many lodge operators are from Europe, where cooking is a fine art, and they are familiar with world cuisines including Chinese, Japanese, Thai and Indian. Most visitors are affluent Americans and Europeans who are accustomed to a light, health-conscious style of cooking, and who find typical Costa Rican fare, with its emphasis on meat and overcooked vegetables, to be unhealthful (many Costa Rican lodges cater specifically for health-conscious travelers).

In expert hands, the results can be delightful. The most memorable meals I've had in Costa Rica fall into this category. A hypothetical dinner, served buffet-style, might include things like: chicken marinated with fresh papayas and mangos and grilled; chicken or lean beef lightly stir-fried with ginger and sesame; a medley of fresh vegetables, lightly cooked and still crispy, with a hint of curry; salad with hearts of palm in a balsamic vinaigrette sauce; cilantro chutney; fresh local fish, grilled with fresh vegetables; another type of fish, prepared as a *ceviche*; mango pie and other fruit-based desserts. Two lodges that execute this culinary tradition well are **Silver King Lodge** in Barra del Colorado, and **Iguana Lodge** in the Peninsula de Osa.

Costa Rican Dishes (*comida típica*)

agua dulce - sweet, hot water consumed like coffee or tea

arreglados - greasy pastries with meat or cheese

arroz con leche - rice pudding

arroz con pollo - fried rice with chicken

batido - fruit smoothie made with either milk or water and ice

bocas - snacks, usually served in bars to accompany beer inducing patrons to buy even more beer to go with the bocas

casado - The archetypal Costa Rican dish is a plate lunch (or dinner) consisting of a choice of meat or fish with a large number of vegetable side items usually including plantains, rice, beans, cabbage, corn, and fruit. A casado is usually the best way to sample local food at reasonable prices.

casava - a large, potato-like root vegetable with a fairly plain flavor

ceviche - marinated seafood, "cooked" by lime juice, not by heat

chan - a strange slimy drink made from weird seeds

chorreados - corn pancakes, usually served with sour cream

chuleta - chop

chicharones - fried pork skins

coyol - palm wine, exceedingly dangerous

elote - corn on the cob

empanadas - turnovers with beans, cheese, meat, or potatoes

enchiladas - pastries with cheese and potatoes or meat

gallo pinto - "Spotted rooster" is usually served at breakfast and consists of last night's leftover rice and beans stir fried with garlic, onions and whatever is on hand. Delicious!

guaro - very potent local hooch made from sugar

hígado en salsa - liver in sauce

horchata - a cinnamon-flavored drink made with corn or rice

mondongo - soup made from beef stomach

olla de carne - beef stew

palmitos - heart of palm

patacones - fried plantains

pinolillo - a hot drink made from chocolate and corn

plantain - a large, fat, unsweet banana usually fried and served with meals.

queque - cake

resbaladera - a drink made from barley and rice

tres leches - a sweet cake drenched in sweet milk, delicious!

No Costa Rican meal is complete without a dash of *Lizano* sauce. You'll find a bottle of this delicious tamarind-based condiment on the table at every restaurant. Vaguely similar to Worcestershire (but lighter) or to the Jamaican Pickapeppa, *salsa Lizano* makes the perfect companion to *gallo pinto*, but goes well with almost any savory dish. Ticos go through the stuff by the gallon, and the founder of the company that makes it is said to be one of Costa Rica's richest men.

Costa Rican coffee is excellent. I like a *café con leche*, which tends to be about half milk. If you want black coffee, ask for *café negro*.

Beer is brewed in the German lager tradition. Local brands such as **Imperial** (*águila* in local slang) and the hearty **Bavaria** are very good.

Wine is, of course, not produced in the tropics, so most Costa Ricans aren't big wine drinkers. Imported wine (often from Chile) is available in stores and at upscale restaurants, but it's expensive, and the selection is usually limited.

Rum, distilled from sugar, is the typical tropical liquor. There's a variety of brands available, ranging from basic mixing rum to fine, dark sipping rum. Rum and Coke (*Cuba Libre*) is Costa Rica's most popular mixed drink.

Some of the locals drink *guaro*, a clear liquor distilled from sugarcane. Similar to moonshine or to Jamaican "overproof" rum, guaro is very cheap and very strong. You have been warned.

Whatever you eat in Costa Rica, do not neglect to sample some of whatever fruits are in season. The mangos, pineapples, papayas, bananas, citrus and other tropical delights that grow down here are simply different fruits from the ones you buy at the supermarket back home: sweet, juicy and cheap. Fresh-squeezed juices from a rainbow of exotic fruits are available everywhere. Don't be afraid to experiment.

TELEPHONES

The telephone system is a little on the crummy side, but serviceable. Cell phones are common, and you can even rent one for your visit.

The country code is 506. To call Costa Rica from the US, dial: 011 506 [local number].

In 2008, the phone company added another digit to all Costa Rican phone numbers. All numbers now have eight digits. If you run across a seven-digit number (and you will, considering how seldom many companies update their web sites and brochures), you must add a "2" before the number if it's a landline, or an "8" if it's a cell phone. Hope it works!

Most phone booths use phone cards, which you can buy at grocery stores and newsstands. **Phone cards** are a bargain, and offer the cheapest way to call North America. Phone cards can be purchased in most local grocery stores (*pulperías*) in denominations from $1 on up. Local calls are only a couple of cents using these cards and calls to the US are pretty cheap. The cards work with most touch-tone phones except for some of the older public phones.

Another good way to call home is by calling the direct access number for your long-distance company, and using your calling card:

• **AT&T**: *Tel. 0800 011 4114*
• **MCI**: *Tel. 0800 012 2222*
• **Sprint**: *Tel. 0800 013 0123*

To call the US or Canada from Costa Rica, dial 001 [area code and number].

Avoid making calls from hotels, which love to add a hefty markup to the price. Many remote lodges are far from phone lines or cellular coverage, so the only option may be to use a satellite phone, which is quite expensive.

You can send **faxes** at most post offices and hotels.

Blue "tourist phones" are starting to show up at hotels and some tourist attractions. These are clearly marked as being particularly for calls overseas and take only credit cards. Although convenient and easy to use, they are extremely expensive, with even short calls to the US running over $30. Avoid them.

TIME

The time in Costa Rica is **equal to US Central Standard Time** (six hours behind Greenwich Mean Time, one hour behind Eastern Standard Time). However, they do not recognize Daylight Savings Time. The length of the days and nights doesn't vary much here in the tropics. It gets dark about 6pm every day, year round. Nicaragua tried Daylight Savings Time a couple of years ago but dropped it as almost everyone simply ignored it.

TIPPING

A **10% service charge is added to all restaurant bills**, so there's no need to do more than round up to the next even amount, unless service is exceptional. Taxi drivers don't usually expect tips. Porters should receive a little something. Many tour guides have come to expect tips, especially in tourist-swamped regions such as Monteverde, but you really needn't give them anything extra unless they go above and beyond the call of duty.

You may occasionally be approached by freelance porters, usually young kids (in a former age, they would have been called "blackguard boys") who hang around tourist areas and offer to carry your bags, guard your car while you're away, help you through the intricacies of buying a bus ticket, or other small services. Use your discretion as to whether they are to be trusted. If your tip is too small, they'll let you know.

TOURIST INFORMATION

The **Costa Rica Tourist Board** has lots of information on their Web site, including visa and entry requirements, customs, flights, hotels, tours, car rental and more, plus lots of maps and photos. *Info: Instituto Costarricense de Turismo, www.visitcostarica.com; Tel. 866/COSTARICA.*

WATER

Tap water in larger cities is theoretically safe to drink, although **I recommend sticking to bottled water to be safe**. Remote lodges may have dodgy water supplies, with low pressure and little or no hot water.

WEIGHTS & MEASURES

All measurements in Costa Rica use the metric system. Liquids are sold by the liter, which is a tiny bit more than a quart. Food is often sold by the gram. One kilogram is 2.2 pounds, and 100 grams of meat or cheese is about enough for a sandwich. Distance is measured in meters (about 39 inches) or kilometers (1.6 kilometers equals 1 mile). Temperature is measured in Celsius degrees. 0° Celsius is freezing, or 32° Fahrenheit. 100° Celsius equals the boiling point of water, or 212° F. Most people you'll meet in the tourist industry are familiar with our American system of measurement, so they will usually be able to give you a rough-and-ready conversion. One hundred kilometers is roughly 60 miles. If the posted speed limit is 80 km/hr, that means 48 mph. If the speed limit is 100, (rare in Costa Rica), that means 60 mph.

WEB SITES

Be very careful about information you find on web sites. Many companies (and government agencies) never update their sites. You'll find beautiful sites for hotels and tour operators that went out of business a decade ago. Always call, or check out the latest posts on *www.tripadvisor.com*.

- *www.visitcostarica.com*. The official site of the Costa Rica Tourist Board has lots of good general information. There's also an excellent database of hotels and tour operators.
- *www.ticotimes.net*. This is the site of the English-language Tico Times.
- *www.nacion.com*. The site of the largest local newspaper.
- *www.ecotourism.org*. The site of the International Ecotourism Society includes lists of environmentally friendly lodges and tour operators.
- *www.costaricamapproject.com*. This site has a couple of handy specialized maps.
- *www.arcr.net*. This is a resource for those living in Costa Rica or considering moving there.

Costa-Rica-oriented search engines:
- *www.bruncas.com*
- *www.cibercentro.com/costarica*
- *www.dmoz.org/Regional/Central_America/Costa_Rica/*

Privately-operated sites with varying amounts of useful information:
- *www.costarica.com*
- *www.costaricabureau.com*
- *www.costa-rica-guide.com*
- *www.costarica-nationalparks.com*
- *www.costaricamap.com*

ESSENTIAL SPANISH
Pleasantries
Please - *por favor*
Thank you - *gracias*
You're welcome - *de nada*
Excuse me - *perdóneme or permiso or discúlpeme*
Good day - *buenos días*
Good night - *buenas noches*
Goodbye - *adiós*
Hello - *hola*
How are you? - *¿Cómo está usted? or ¿Qué tal?*
Fine - *muy bien*
Pleased to meet you - *mucho gusto*

Everyday Phrases
Yes - *sí*
No - *no*
I don't know - *No sé*
Do you speak English? - *¿Habla usted inglés?*
I don't speak Spanish. - *Yo no hablo español*
Friend – *amigo*
Where? - *¿Donde?*
When? - *¿Cuando?*
Why? - *¿Porqué?*
How much? - *¿Cuanto?*
How do you say… - *¿Cómo se dice…?*
Today - *hoy*
Tomorrow - *mañana*
I would like - *quisiera*
Here - *aquí*
There - *allá*
More - *más*
Less - *menos*

Much - *mucho*
Little - *poco*
Large - *grande*
Small - *pequeño*
Good - *bueno*
Bad - *malo*
What a deal! - *¡Que ganga!*

Travel Terms
Hotel - *(el) hotel*
Bank - *(el) banco*
Money - *(el) dinero*
Airport - *(el) aeropuerto*
Taxi - *(el) taxi*
Bus - *(el) autobús, camioneta*
Car - *(el) coche, carro*
Bathrooms - *(los) baños*
Gas station - *(la) bomba, gasolinera*
How far is . . . - *¿Qué distancia es . . . ?*
Road, highway - *(la) carretera*

Eating & Drinking (*comer y tomar*)
Meat - *(la) carne*
Beef - *(el) bistec*
Pork - *(el) cerdo*
Chicken - *(el) pollo*
Fish - *(el) pescado*
Seafood - *(los) mariscos*
Shrimp - *(los) camarones*
Vegetables - *(los) legumbres*
Fruits - *(las) frutas*
Pineapple - *(la) piña*
Banana - *(el) plátano, banano*
Orange - *(la) naranja*
Apple - *(la) manzana*
Blackberry - *(la) mora*
Guava - *(la) guayaba*
Water - *(el) agua*
Milk - *(la) leche*
Coffee - *(el) café*

Tea - *(el) té*
Beer - *(la) cerveza*
Red Wine/White Wine - *vino tinto/vino blanco*
Glass (of water) - *(la) taza de agua*
Glass of wine - *(la) copa de vino*
Soft drink - *(el) refresco*
Smoothie - *(el) batido*
Juice - *(el) jugo*

Costa Rican Terms
Águila - slang name for Imperial beer, after the eagle on the label
Beneficio - coffee factory
Bomba - gas station
Buena nota - good, OK
Chapulines - youth gangs
Chepe - local name for San José
Chorizo - bribe (literally, a sausage)
Chunche - thing
¡Qué chuso! - cool!
¿Cómo amaneció? - How did you wake up? Used for "good morning."
Fauna silvestre - wildlife
Ganja - marijuana (actually Jamaican slang)
Guaro - local cane liquor
Hora americana - more or less on time
Hora tica - mañana time
Mae, Maje - "dummy," used in a nice, kidding way like "pal"
María - taxi meter
Mota - marijuana
Pulpería - small grocery store
Precarista - squatter
¡Pura vida! - all-purpose interjection (literally, "pure life")
Sendero - nature trail
Soda - luncheonette or small restaurant
Tico(a) - Costa Rican person
¡Upé! - Is anyone home? (used instead of knocking)

Pronunciation
It's important to have a basic idea of pronunciation, so you can pronounce place names correctly.

Spanish is a phonetic language, meaning that words are almost always spelled just as they sound. Vowels are pronounced roughly as follows:

- a - as in *father*
- e - between *e* in *get* and *a* in *same*
- i - as in *magazine*
- o - as in *phone*
- u - as in *prune*

There are no silent vowels. For example, *coche* (car) is pronounced KO-chay. A written accent on a vowel means that it is stressed, as in San José (pronounced sahn ho-SAY).

Consonants are pronounced roughly the same as in English, except:

- c - like *k* before *a*, *o* or *u*; like *s* before *e* or *i*
- h - always silent
- j - like *h* in *home*
- ll - like *y* in *yet*
- ñ - like *ni* in *union*
- s - always hard, as in *soda* (never soft, as in *ease*)
- z - like *s*

INDEX

THINGS CHANGE!

Phone numbers, prices, addresses, quality of service – all change. If you come across any new information, let us know. No item is too small! Contact us at :

jopenroad@aol.com

or

www.openroadguides.com

TravelNotes

TravelNotes

TravelNotes

MAP & PHOTO CREDITS

Maps: All maps except San Jose map by Charlie Morris; San Jose map by design-maps.com.

Photos: Bruce Morris: p. 62; Silver King Lodge: p. 65; Río Parismina Lodge: p. 70; Manatus Lodge: p. 73.

Open Road Publishing